I0009138

3D Realism
Practical & Easy Workflows ©

First manual series

3D Realism
Practical & Easy Workflows ©

First manual series

Jamie Cardoso

Copyrights

© 2011 3D Realism Practical & Easy Workflows. All rights reserved.

No part of this publication may be reproduced or transmitted in any form or by any means, electronic or mechanical, including photocopying, recording, or any information storage and retrieval system, without permission in writing from the Author.

Requests to the Author for permission should be addressed to jamiecardo@hotmail.com

This book and its contents are protected by the Copyright Licensing Agency.

Warning and Disclaimer

Every effort was made to make this book as complete and as accurate as possible, but no warranty or fitness is implied. The information provided is on an "as is" basis. The Author shall have neither liability nor responsibility to any loss or damages arising from the information contained in this book.

© 2011 3D Realism Practical & Easy Workflows. All rights reserved.

Book Contributors

Graham Macfarlane	Senior 3D Visualiser
Andrew Gibbon	Senior 3D Visuliser
Martins Cardoso	IT Strategist

Contents

Contents

Project Files

Please visit: http://3drealism-easyworkflows.com/companions/allfiles/download/index

Alternatively, email: jamiecardo@hotmail.com to report any problems with the book or the URL.

Bonus Scene
Completed and ready to render VRay project Scene

Main Project Files for:

Chapter 1: Pre-Production

Chapter 2: Production

Chapter 3: Post-Production

Preface

While it's important to know of all "the right buttons to press" in order to overcome software issues; an artist's final image will ultimately be judged on its own merits.

Similarly, having an amazing portfolio with one's personal work is not always an assurance that most of one's commercial work will be equally great. Indeed, there are only few fortunate individuals and companies with the knowledge and the skills to consistently produce outstanding work in real projects.

This first manual series will provide users with a unique insight into the crafty process of consistently producing striking 3D Visuals.

The step-by-step tutorials are project focused and designed to help intermediate/advanced users raise their existing skills to the next level, by simply meticulously following three easy steps: Pre-Production, Production & Post-Production.

These three unique chapters will cover in detail subjects such as: Compositing, modelling, importing files, applying shaders, textures, using modifiers, lighting, rendering and much more.

All tutorials have useful tips and tricks throughout, coupled with theories and analyses of each technique implemented.

The Project scenes were created for 3Ds Max/Design 2010 and above, using mental ray. There's also a completed project scene for **VRay** and numerous PSD example files.

Acknowledgments

I would like to acknowledge my uncle Richard Bobb and my brother Martins Cardoso who have been my greatest supporters.
Also, I would like to thank my listed friends and colleagues who have given me valuable tips throughout the entire process:
Geof Chilvers, Olivier Ladeuix, Andrew Gibbon, Nadeen Bhatti, Graham Macfarlane and Elitsa.

Finally, I would like to dedicate this book to my family.

Jamie Cardoso

The Author

Jamie is a senior computer Artist/Technologist/Author/Reviewer, whose first-rate experience was gained designing and producing work for a wide range of clients worldwide.

Much of Jamie's work and contributions had been featured in books; and magazines such as 3D World Magazine, CG Society and 3D Total, to name but a few.

He is also the co-author of two successful books entitled: Realistic Architectural Visualization with 3Ds Max and mental ray.

Jamie regularly shares his expert knowledge with users by constantly updating his blog.

http://jamiecardoso-mentalray.blogspot.com/

Google: jamie cardoso

Office Rendering

Chapter 1
Pre-Production

1.1 Introduction

It's common practice to establish from the start: the type of project involved; the target audience and the media platform/s in which the final product is to be showcased on.

Projects can range from a simple design exercise for a PDF/PowerPoint presentation; to high end marketing images for magazines, newspaper, billboards, TV, etc.

Design exercises or renders for PDF/PowerPoint documents, do not require the same level of expertise and precision as marketing images.

Marketing image gurus have in fact concluded that, it's far more difficult to produce compelling images without a clear art direction (i.e. photo references; etc.) than otherwise.

The pre-production phase is designed to help the Studio/Artist and the client to establish the art direction prior to entering the production stage.
When failing to sign off this crucial stage (i.e. pre-production), the final product will be more likely to be exposed to criticism and constant reviews by the client.

Furthermore, it may subsequently result in "stretched" budgets and unfulfilled expectations by both: the client and the Artist/Studio.

The following tutorial will take you through the entire process of consistently producing captivating marketing images.

1.2 Research & Development

Creating prestigious marketing images often starts with the initial brief from the client describing their ideas, concepts, textures/finishes, design drafts, vision, photo reference, etc.

Photo References for Finishes & Lighting

With all the information supplied, one should begin making preliminary decisions with regards to finding the best photo references to use for art direction, design possibilities, lighting, finishes, etc. This process is considered be one of the most important stages of the pre-production, as the artist/s/studio will liaise directly with the client about the following:

1. The most relevant features of the project/design.
This will later prove crucial when setting up the cameras and the composition.

2. Find out the story behind the design/project. This may also play an important role in deciding: the composition, the overall lighting rig/mood, the types of people to be added in post, and how people should interact with the space/shot, and with each other.

3. The media platform that the marketing image will be displayed on (i.e. Magazines, Billboards, TV, Newspaper, etc.).
This process is fundamental when selecting the types photo references, as it will have a direct impact on the choice of the 3d contents, colour, camera position, render output size, etc.

4. Other alternative art directions. This process involves having numerous photo references representing other dynamic camera positions, composition, lighting, colours, colour scheme, materials/finishes, etc, that may benefit the final image.
As mentioned earlier, this is the stage where the artist/studio should source for numerous striking photo references relevant to the criteria (i.e. similar spaces, structures, design, media platform and ideas) to help the client decide the art direction- Mood Boards.
Most of these striking photos can easily be sourced from websites such as Flickr; Books; etc.

Mood Boards

1.3 Camera & Composition

The following step is for the artist/studio to create draft/low poly 3d versions of the most relevant items of the 3d composition.
These should be based on sketches/drawings and photos supplied by the client. Alternatively, one can use the 3d model supplied, if available.

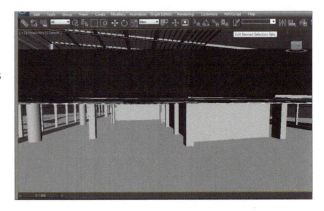

3D Model from Client

Printed Drawing with Camera Positions

Next, one can start setting up the camera positions that encompass the relevant areas of the design, according based on the previous information supplied, and the photo references sourced by the artist.

With help from the artist/studio, the client should sketch out the camera position/s, and the field of view (FOV); preferably on a 2d drawing print.

This is a good technique to quickly assess where the camera/s should be placed.
The camera position and its settings play a crucial role in producing the final render.
It is very important at this early stage to decide how one wants the final image to be interpreted through the camera lens (i.e. in an artistic, cinematic or standard photography manner).
Even untrained eyes can quickly assess whether or not an image is realistic, based on how the camera is positioned or setup.
The camera's FOV (i.e. field of view) should reflect the values commonly used in real cameras, coupled with appropriate render output size to help capture the scene's essence (portrait/landscape). The final result should be based on how well the camera, the scene and its contents complement each other in a dramatic and effective way.

Having the camera at eye level (i.e. 1.60m) or another realistic position is important for two main reasons:

1. Our eyes can easily spot odd camera positions (i.e. unusual height/position).

2. Having the camera at eye level will facilitate integrating people, and other objects in post.

At times, even accurate scenes may look disproportionate, as result of not having the camera at eye level.

Professionals often create the original camera type as "Target" to set its direction. Once that is done, the camera is then immediately changed to "Free Camera" type, for more flexibility in moving/rotating the camera in the viewport.

Also, there's an interesting software called "Beam your Screen"; which helps clients to have a direct/interactive input,

Creating a Target Camera

during the creation of the 3D camera. It does it by allowing the client to remotely "tap" into the artist's computer screen, and interactively observe the camera being created. This process will help the artist/studio to quickly pick and set key camera views for the client.

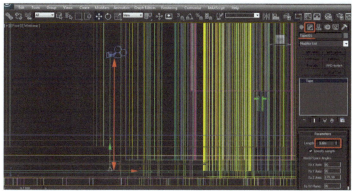

Camera at Eye Level

Setting up the Camera Output Size

"Signing off" the shot/ composition also involves going backwards and forwards with the client, while deciding on the geometry that should be in the foreground and background.

1.4 Previewing the Art Direction

During the process of establishing the final art direction, you will be required to "Photoshop" elements such as photos, notes, sketches and other effects on top of the previously taken screen grab, or a draft render. The final result should be an artist's impression, or a collage depicting the overall art direction of the final shot.

The entire exercise is designed to help the client quickly understand and preview the impact of their choices based on the design and the artistic decisions previously made.

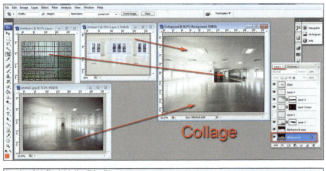

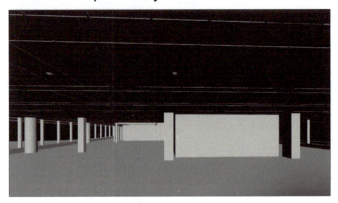

Draft Render of the Camera Shot for Collage

Creating a Collage preview of the Final Result

It's also worth mentioning that, while liaising with the client, one should be adventurous by trying to break the mould, and suggest new ideas and effects such as:

. Vignetting

. Subtle surface discrepancies

. Chromatic aberration (…this is the one effect that you should not mention to the client, but simply add it in a very subtle manner).

. Depth of field (it is mostly relevant when there are objects in the foreground)

. Glow

. Lens Flare

. Dynamic camera positions

. ETC

All the above mentioned steps will aid the client when reviewing the overall budget and the final art direction.
It will also help avoid the usual project constraints related to lighting, composition, textures/finishes; final quality, etc.

1.5 Detail Modelling, Positioning Objects, and Camera

As previously mentioned, the usage of references (i.e. drawings, photos, etc) is very important when selecting and modelling realistic objects.

One should concentrate mainly in detailing objects that are closer to the camera. Objects in the distance often look acceptable with a nice and simple texture, and bump/displacement applied to their respective shaders.

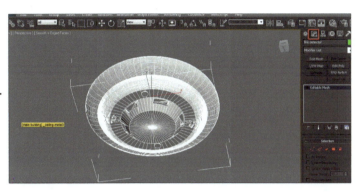

Detail Modelling

It's also important to model and scale 3d objects realistically. Setting up the metric units' scale is a good starting point.

It's good practice to always look for references of scale between objects in 2D drawings, photos and around you.

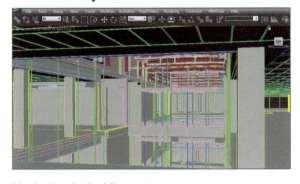

Navigating in the Viewport

When creating and adding detailed geometry in the scene, it's worth finding an efficient way of navigating in the viewport; by occasionally displaying the less relevant objects as boxes(i.e. box display mode). This technique is to speed up the viewport performance whilst navigating and creating the 3d scene.

Although not always necessary, creating proxies is another method of working and rendering efficiently.

1.6 Importing/Merging 3D Models

When sourcing or using 3d models from a third party, it is worth testing them in a separate file for possible missing bitmaps; to change crucial parameters; to check for potential bugs or renderering conversion errors.

The internal bugs may manifest themselves as "black splotches" on renders; ridiculously slow render times; etc.

These bugs are often created accidently during the process of converting scenes across 3d platforms; through switching rendering engines or a malicious act by another user.

In some extreme circumstances users may find themselves having to individually render hundreds of different objects in order to detect the "rogue" object/s.

The precautionary measures mentioned earlier will later prove crucial when finalizing your project.

1.7 Importing DWGs

When importing 2D drawings (i.e. DWGs) into the main 3d software, it's crucial to do the following:

1. Ensure to have the original 2d drawing completely "cleaned/stripped" from AutoCAD or Micro Station (i.e. omit unnecessary text and other layers). This procedure will reduce the size of the incoming file.

2. Most drawings are originally created far away from the 0.0.0 point. Since 3Ds Max and most 3d applications have difficulty displaying/representing lines or objects accurately at such distances, it's imperative to reposition the drawings as close to 0.0.0 point as possible, prior to importing them into the 3d application.
Some of the well known difficulties are the inability to create straight lines and accurate lights.

3. There are a number of techniques that professionals use to move the drawings.
One popular technique is to first create a dummy/point/line at 0.0.0 point.
followed by selecting the drawing layers from the file; and move/snap them onto the previously created dummy/point/line (i.e. at 0.0.0 point).

4. Once the drawings are close to the 0.0.0 point; it's important to save out the file under a different name, to prevent overwriting the original file.
At times, one may be required to explode and attach objects in AutoCAD, to ensure that bjects/lines are imported without artifacts.

5. In MicroStation, one is required to select the "Fence" tool; followed by drawing a rectangle around the desired area, and typing in the " FF=" command, to save out the drawing under a different name.
Note that, MicroStation is set to automatically save the file, every time a change is made to a drawing. For this reason one is required to "Fence" save first, prior to moving/snapping the drawings onto the dummy line/point/object.
The DGN (i.e. MicroStation) file has to be saved as a DWG, prior to being imported into the main 3d software.

6. When the drawings are "stripped/cleaned" and moved to 0.0.0 point or closer; one can begin importing the file/s into the main 3d software.

Before importing the drawing/s into the main 3d software, it's important to choose the metric system setup (i.e. millimeters, meters, etc); as opposed to keeping the default system to "Generic Units".

Also one needs to set the system to "Respect System Units in Files". These two functions will be vital in ensuring that incoming files are not disproportionate in size and/or automatically re-scaled.

Units Setup Parameters

AutoCad DWG/DXF Import Options

7. When importing the drawing, it's important to pay extra attention to the "Model Scale" group, in the "AutoCad DWG/DFX Import Options" dialog box. The "Incoming file units" function should be left untouched.

And either enable or disable the "Rescale" function, depending on the total value of the "Resulting model size".

The rule of thumb is to always choose the smaller metric value displayed in the "Resulting model" size" text field, when enabling or disabling the "Rescale" function. Once the drawings are in the 3d scene, check the dimensions with the "Tape" helper.

Also, the "Curve steps" values should be increased if smooth curves of the incoming drawings are faceted. This function will increase the number of vertices in faceted areas.

9. Next, select the entire drawing, and group it. It's common practice to name the group in accordance to its original name (i.e. DWG_floor plan_5th floor).

In addition, it is also important to create a layer under a similar name.

Professionals often work with layers due to its ease of use, and the overall flexibility it provides to control the contents of the entire scene.

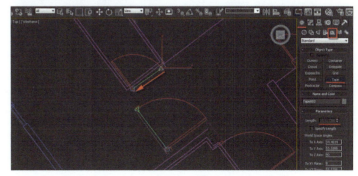

Checking the drawing Dimensions with the Tape helper

To create a layer, simply click on the "Create New Layer" button.
Most users tend to select an object in scene first; followed by creating the layer thereafter.
This is to ensure that, the selected object is automatically added/moved into the newly created layer.
Otherwise, one can simply deselect all objects in the scene, and create a new empty layer in the dialog box.

One can do the following with the layers: select the layer as a group; select individual objects from its content list; turn it on/off; freeze; etc.

Select from Scene dialog

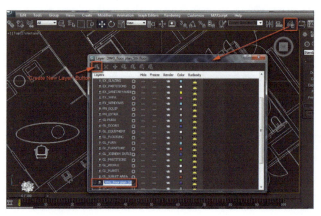

Layer tool dialog

When a layer/folder is created, and the objects are automatically moved into this newly created layer/folder. The main "Layer" dialog box list will still retain the unused copies of the object's name/s in its list.
These unused names/layers can be found in the root of the dialog box, or inside another layer/folder.
It is also common for professionals to delete all unused layers/objects from the list, in order to clean/tidy up the dialog box.

The layer under the name of "0(default)" is the default layer created automatically. This layer can not be deleted.
If the user doesn't manually create a new layer/folder, most objects created in the scene will be automatically added/moved into this default layer/folder.
Although one can select and move the contents of this default layer/folder, users are unable to delete it (i.e. "0(default)", even when empty.

It is worth noting that, users are only able to delete empty layers/folders.

To edit, move or delete layers/folders, one has to select it/them from the dialog list first.

To rename a layer/folder from the list, simply double click it, followed by typing in a name.

When naming the layer/s, it is important to add a number next to the name (i.e. "3D_DWG_Ceiling...").This is mainly to ensure that layers of relevance always stay on top of the list; as it can easily be overlooked/lost among the other layers.

1.8 Setting up the Scene for Modelling

Naming a Layer

1. Set up the snap tools parameters and the toggle to 2.5(2d).
Since the drawings are in 2d (i.e. splines), professionals usually change the "Snaps Toggle" from the default "3" to "2.5", by simply left clicking and holding down its icon, on the main toolbar.

To quickly snap the splines whilst tracing the drawing, one is required to change some key parameters:
Right click on the "Snaps Toggle" icon from the main toolbar. Its dialog box should pop up.

Snaps Toggle   *Snaps Toggle at 2.5*

Enable the "Vertex" and "Endpoint" functions. Also in the "Options" tab, enable the "Snap to frozen objects" function. This will ensure that even frozen splines can be traced and snapped onto.

2. Create a grid by opening the "Helpers" command. Select the "Grid" command and drag the cursor across the viewport. Always choose the corner of a drawing, followed by snapping and dragging the cursor along the viewport.

Vertex & Endpoint functions   *Snap to frozen objects*

3. Exit the creation by first releasing the mouse, and right clicking thereafter.
Next, rotate and snap the grid to align perfectly (i.e. 100%) to the corners of the drawing.

4. Once aligned, right click on the selected grid and choose to activate it.
Once the grid is activated, choose the top grid viewport; by first right clicking on the top viewport text; selecting the "Grid" option from the list, and choosing the "Top" grid view.

Snapping the Grid Helper

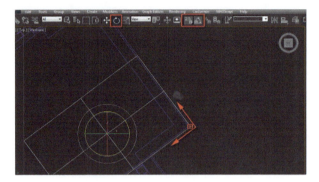

Aligning the Grid

Activate Grid

Grid View: Top

The drawing should automatically rotate and position itself correctly. The grid tool is ideal when working with rotated drawings.

This way one is not required to rotate the drawing/s individually.

The grid helper can also be very useful when setting Max to automatically create objects at a certain height level (i.e. 2.5 m) without having to manually move the objects from the 0.0.0 point. To do so, simply move the grid to the desired height level, in the left or right viewport.

Before moving/rotating the grid, ensure to deactivate it, and set the view to normal viewport (i.e. not grid view).

Once finished moving and rotating the grid helper, simply activate it again.

If you desire to start tracing lines in the "Front" viewport, simply create a grid in the front viewport. Since drawings are produced as plans, elevations and sections; professionals often have to work with a variety of grid helpers, for different height levels, and in different viewports.

5. Another important feature to enable is the "Zoom About Mouse Point (orthographic)" function. This function will help you follow the mouse cursor whilst creating the spline (i.e. tracing), and by occasionally pressing on the "I" key, and "Z" key.

This technique is crucial to implement when creating splines continuously across the viewport.

To enable it, simply click on the "Customize" tab of the main toolbar first. On the dropdown list, choose the "Preferences" option.

In the preferences dialog, under the "Mouse Control" group, enable the "Zoom About Mouse Point (orthographic)".

Preferences

Zoom About Mouse Point

6. It's also important to set a key shortcut to freeze selected objects. This will enable users to freeze objects from opened groups, without the need to close the group first.

Professionals often resort to this key shortcut in order to have better control over the objects being selected in the scene; especially when working in complex 3d files.

To access this dialog simply click on the "Customize" tab, and choose the "Customize User Interface" option from the list. Its dialog should open.In the "Action" list, scroll down to select the "Freeze Selection" option. In the "Hotkey" function, type in "Ctrl+F" keys, and click "Assign" to apply it.

7. It's equally important to set the "Orbit" tool to rotate the viewport around the axis of the selected object.

Customize User Interface

Freeze Selection hotkey

Choosing the Orbit Selected tool

Orbit Selected

Orbit Selected enabled

8. Also, set 3Ds Max to show the most commonly used "Modify" buttons such as Extrude; UVW map, etc.

Doing this will save users time, by not having to constantly search and pick commonly used modifiers in the "Modify" dropdown list menu. To customize and display the modifier buttons, simply click and hold down the "Configure Modifier Sets" button, and choose the same from the pop up list. In the dialog, drag and drop your commonly used modifiers from the list, onto the "Modifiers" group buttons (i.e. add & replace). Also, scroll down the list to pick other useful modifiers. Once finished, close the dialog and set the "Configure Modifier Sets to "Show Buttons".

Configure Modifier Sets   Adding Modifier Buttons

1.9 Shaders and Textures

By default some of the shader parameters' are either too high or too low; and other parameters need to be enabled or disabled, occasionally. Shaders and textures are the second most important aspects of a render.

Show Buttons

Prior to starting, as previously discussed, it's important to have all the relevant photo references at one's disposal and set the Gamma LUT/Correction correctly in your Max scene.

The shaders and textures should reflect the physical properties depicted in the photo references. One should focus mainly in physical properties such as glossiness (i.e. shine), reflectivity, transparency, colour, corner edges, bump/displacement values, and how they react to light.

1. Glossy highlights, reflective objects and displacement/bump maps are some of the major contributors in making an image more appealing!

Most striking photos contain highlights generated from: Direct illumination; from an environment map(i.e. HDRI; etc), or other glossy and reflective objects in the scene.

So whenever possible it's useful to incorporate these effects in the render.

Reflections often turn a "dull" scene into a very interesting one, depending on the content of the reflections.

Glossy highlights and Reflective objects

2. The "Round Corners" function also plays a crucial role in making objects more appealing. Most objects around us are chamfered. So it makes sense to incorporate this effect on materials.

The "Fillet Radius" results can only be previewed in the render.

To find out the correct value to enter without having to test render; artists often create a "dummy" chamfered geometry (i.e. chamfered box from extended primitives) of similar size to one's object. Followed by tweaking with its fillet values to preview the results in the viewport.
Once satisfied with the results, simply enter the value in material parameters, and hide/delete the "dummy" chamfered box primitive.

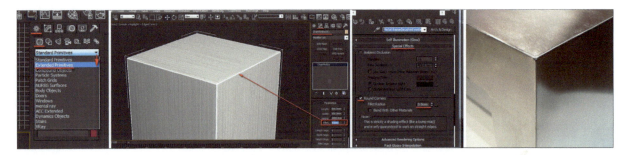

Round Corners

3. Textures are equally important, as its appearance need to be accurate (i.e. correct colour; tiling; sharpness; etc.).
One of the best techniques to achieve realistic textures is to use real photos taken from the respective surface. These photos need to encompass large areas of the desired surface.

For instance, if one's intention is to texture a simple floor; professionals would often take vertically & horizontally precise photo/s of the intended surface, capturing large portions of it (without any direct shadows). And later assign it directly onto the 3d surface.

This technique will reduce the amount of Photoshop work required when omitting repetitive patterns. And also help capture all the nice details such as subtle dust elements; occlusion details; scratches; irregular surface undulations; etc.

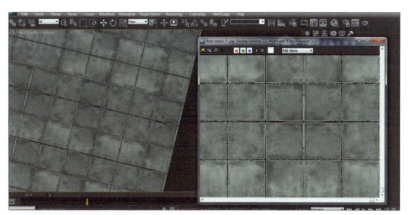

A Photo capturing Large portions of the tiled surface

For quick results, it's common practice to initially apply the basic shader parameters and textures; followed by test rendering them...when necessary, without any pre calculations or lights.

Another good technique to match specific texture tile sizes (i.e. tiles; planks; etc.) is to do the following:

In the shaded top viewport, create or draw a square/rectangle shape with the specified dimension/s of the tile size (i.e. 1200x1200 mm).

Followed by matching the texture tile dimensions, while tweaking with its UVW coordinates.

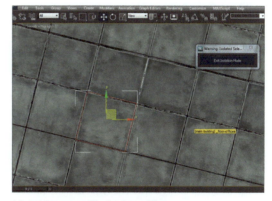

Matching specific texture Sizes

Note that, since the original photo texture/s are the true representation of the surface, everything should fit seemingly.

All other parameters such as bump/displacement values; reflections; glossiness; etc, should be looked at (tweaked) later, when the lighting and other global parameters are being refined.

A further refinement should be made to the shaders and textures when test rendering at full resolution (i.e. region renders).

This step is to closely assess the physical properties of key objects, prior to sending the final renders.

As a rule of thumb, one should continuously name the shaders/materials according to their original shader creation, and/or object name, to keep the file organized.

Naming Materials

Also, one should create Object ID numbers while the shaders/materials are being assigned.

This process will prove indispensable when adding the Object ID render element/pass.

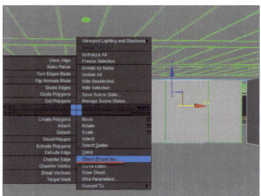

1.10 The Best Approach

Object Properties

Object ID

The next phase is to decide the best, fastest, and the more economical technical approach to execute the project, within the allocated budget and time.

This crucial step will ultimately determine whether or not the budget should be reviewed, along with the deadline.

This evaluation process often involves having to make vital technical & production decisions such as the number of people involved in the project; preferred 3d software; software licences; rendering engine/s; available plug-ins or proprietary ones; team workflow; assessing the best approach between 3d and post production; etc.

3D Software :

Companies often choose the software that they are more comfortable and accustomed to working with; unless there is a specific request to use something alternative or specific.

Also, companies frequently choose the most inclusive software (i.e. the software that most members of the team are familiar with; etc.).
For this project, it was decided that 3Ds max was best suited to achieve the desired results.

Rendering Engine:

Choosing the rendering engine is one of the most crucial technical decisions a company/individual has to make.

At times this decision can cause a major impact on the overall cost of the project (i.e. software licensing; ease of use; turnarounds; reliability; available plug-ins; product support; its integration with the main 3d application and its inclusivity (i.e. the number of team members using it; etc.). For this project, mental ray rendering engine was chosen, for the reasons mentioned above (i.e. free; fully integrated with Max; etc.).

As an artist, I find myself having to switch between rendering engines and 3d applications in order to be flexible, inclusive, convenient and versatile.
In the past, there were even times when I had to use Renderman and Houdini.

For this tutorial, while a 3d software and a rendering engine had to be chosen as a platform; the majority of its content focuses mainly on workflows and general methodologies used by most reputable studios. These techniques can easily be implemented across a variety of 3d applications and rendering engines.

The images depicted below are some of the many which proved to be remarkable. I have produced them while using 3Ds Max and **VRay**, for **TP Bennett Architects**.
These results were only possible by implementing the techniques and workflows described in this book.

Rendering Workflow:

With the rendering engine chosen and the shaders & textures applied, the next step is to plan the quickest and the most efficient method of test rendering progressively towards the big final render:

Setting the Sunlight direction

1. One of the quickest ways to begin test rendering is to set the direction of the sunlight and its colour first.

It's common practice to initially start the test renders with a small image output size. Most global parameters such as image sampling should be also set to draft.

Furthermore, depending on the version of Max and/or the graphics card available, one may be able to interactively see the direction of the sunlight in the viewport, whilst positioning it.

Alternatively, at this early stage, one would have had to switch off the Global Illumination(GI), and apply a basic white, non-reflective material as an override material, in order to speed up the test renders. Also, when using the override material in interior scenes, the glass windows should have the "Cast Shadows" function disabled temporarily, from the object's properties dialog.

This white non-reflective surface is also used to accurately match light colours from photographs, in order to have a "pure" representation of the light colour when hitting the white surface. Therefore, the artist is often required to closely look at white surfaces in the photograph, to determine the original colour of the light/s. It should also be a good opportunity to load in the previously chosen photo reference/s, to help follow the art direction, previously agreed.

2. Once the direction of the sunlight and its colour are set; the next step is to enable the GI; the exposure controls, and begin creating the artificial lights.

The material override function should still be on, and most global parameters should be set to draft.

This approach is often adopted for fast turnarounds, and to quickly assess the overall lighting. Another rule of thumb is avoid using the sky portal, unless absolutely necessary.

While the sky portal is very powerful to redirect and concentrate the sun rays in specific areas of the scene, it can be time consuming to render, at times.

Users often have to increase its shadow samples really high, in order to achieve smooth and clean results (i.e. 32 or higher).

3. When creating the artificial lights, it's wise not to create more lights than necessary.

At times, users feel obliged to create as many artificial lights as indicated on the ceiling plan. Certain floor plans may come with 100, 300 or more, artificial lights.

However, in rendering technical terms it would be "suicidal" to create that many lights in one floor alone.

In such circumstances, the lighting technical director, would normally create and place fewer lights than suggested on the plan. By simply positioning them in crucial and strategic areas of the scene, to try to emulate similar amount of brightness; without straining the computer/s with too many lights.

Creating Artificial Lights with soft shadows

While soft shadows are imperative in the renders, they are also major contributors in increasing the rendering times.

For this reason, professionals often set fewer lights in the scene to cast soft shadows.

All above changes should result in a balanced and nicely lit scene, rendering substantially faster.

While lighting, it's common practice to continuously test render the scene every time a new light is created, or when a fundamental parameter is changed. This will ensure that the scene does not become difficult to manage.

This technique also helps to control the balance of brightness in the scene (i.e. Depth).

Once satisfied with the overall lighting; one can disable the material override function; and begin fine-tuning the final settings of lights; shaders and the textures to react harmoniously in the scene.

So far, it should have been fairly quick to set-up the lights and to test render the scene.

Next, when the shaders, textures, and the lighting are exposed, the image will begin taking slightly longer to render.

This phase may require rendering high resolution regions of the scene, to prevent unexpected results in the final render.

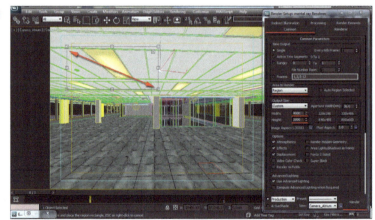

Region Renders

As mentioned earlier, it's imperative to continuously cross-reference between the renders and the photo references to closely match shaders; textures and lights.

The artist should also be conscious of key elements that often make a render appealing, directly from Max:

Highlights and Glossy highlights

Reflections

Diffused Reflections

Diffused glossy highlights

Depth

Highlights and Glossy Highlights

Most striking photos contain all the above mentioned ingredients.

1.11 Harmonious Colour Schemes

Having excellent shaders; lighting; content; etc, may not be sufficient to make a render appealing. Harmony of colours in the scene play an important role in making an image striking.

So whenever possible, one should liaise with the client about object textures and ight colours that may complement the scene.

1.12 Direct and Diffused Shadows

Direct and diffused shadows are ever present in most photos; therefore our eyes expect the presence of both in most images. It is imperative to have these elements in the render when possible.

1.13 Good Design and Detailed Models

While the scale of the 3d models have to be correct, it is also important to have appealing and detailed 3d models in the scene.

Our eyes can easily detect when an object is not detailed enough, therefore perceived unrealistic (i.e. CG). And most critics also have a clear sense of what looks appealing (i.e. round and organic shapes; etc.).

Good Design, Shadows & Harmonious Colours

So one should add as much detail as possible to a 3d model, and select 3d contents that are perceived to be appealing.

1.14 Random Positions

Most striking photos contain objects that are positioned in a natural (i.e. irregular) manner.
In fact, in real life, it's far more difficult to positioned objects in a symmetric way, than otherwise.
So an artist should always try to position 3d objects in a natural and random manner.

1.15 Ambient Occlusion (AO)

The ambient occlusion often helps to "ground" objects in the scene, and create depth.
Therefore, it's important to use it when possible or necessary.

Random Positions

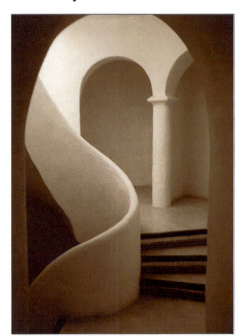

Ambient Occlusion

1.16 Subtle Discrepancies

Our eyes are accustomed to seeing prominent and subtle discrepancies around us (i.e. smudges; scratches; chipped corners; cracks; dirt; irregular bumps; dust; etc.). So when absent in an image, we may subconsciously perceive it to be unnatural (i.e. CG).
For this reason it's important to add these natural discrepancies that our eyes are accustomed to seeing. In 3d visualisation, professionals often add these effects with subtlety.

Subtle Discrepancies

1.17 Distributed Bucket Rendering

This rendering technique enables professionals to use multiple machines (i.e. Hosts) without the need to load the 3d scenes in the respective machines(i.e. Hosts).
While DBR is faster than NetRendering, it's only recommended for still images.
This rendering technique is also very useful when working on large scenes, as the main file will not be loaded in the host's system. However, whilst rendering, one cannot vacate or switch off the main rendering machine, without having to cancel the entire rendering process.

To partially override this inconvenience, professionals often use the "Windows Task Manager" to set the number of processors (CPUs) assigned to the rendering task. To do this simply go to: windows task manager dialog> processes> set affinity> right click on the max.exe >processor affinity>. This windows function lists the number of CPUs your computer is using to process the render. Prior to using the DBR, ensure that all your files (FG Map, bitmaps, file output path, etc.) are in a shared network drive. (…Not local drives such as C, etc.).

Distributed Bucket Rendering

To find out the IP addresses to type in the DBR "name field"; simply do the following:

In the Backburner Queue Monitor, under the "Server" tab, select any server from the list, and right-click. On the dropdown list, choose the "Column Chooser "selection.
The "Server Columns" dialog will appear. Select and drag the "IP Address" tab from the "Server Columns" dialog and drop it into the "Backburner Queue Monitor", under the "Server" tab.
This will allow the user to view all IP address numbers that will be later typed in the name field.

Alternatively, one can go to: **windows start up>type in run>cmd>ipconfig** of each machine to be assigned to the DBR. It's commendable to pre-save and freeze any Global Illumination calculations, otherwise the rendered frames, regions/crops will differ in results.

It's imperative for users to install similar software; DLLs; etc; in each assigned machine, prior to begin rendering. Otherwise, rendering errors will occur.

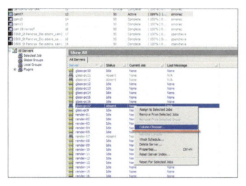

Column Chooser

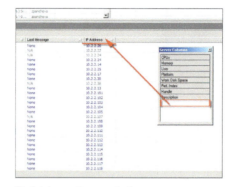

IP Address Server Column

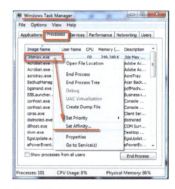

Set Affinity

1.18 Net Render

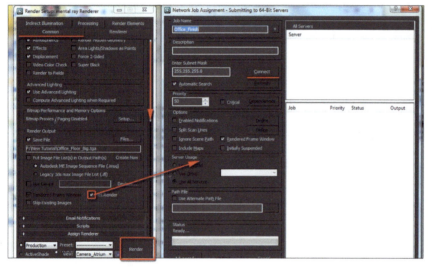

Net Render Dialog

Net render is the process of sending a job/render to one, or multiple computers, from one's machine, to the Backburner in the network.

Some of many advantages of using this rendering technique is the fact that, users can safely assign or remove servers/computers from jobs/renders randomly, whilst the rendering is taking place. This also includes the machine from which the main renders were sent from.

All renders are handled over the network, through the Backburner. In order for any of the assigned machines to pick up the job renders, one is required to launch the "Server" dialog box from each of the assigned computers/machines.

When the server is launched, it automatically loads up the entire Max file, prior to rendering it. Loading huge 3d files may at times generate errors in the Backburner. When using the Backburner, it's imperative for the assigned machines to possess similar software; DLLs; etc; prior to begin rendering. Otherwise, errors will occur.

In addition, users also have the option to use it in conjunction with the DBR. Or use the Net Render with "Split Scan lines" function; set job Dependencies; etc.

1.19 Global parameters

Planning the manner in which the global rendering parameters will be used throughout the project, will play an important role in handling the speed and efficiency of the project.

BSP parameters are one of first parameters to be looked at:

In scenes with over 1.000.000 triangles, users are strongly advised to switch to the BSP2 method, to ensure that the geometry is handled more efficiently. To view the scene's statistics, simply press the "7" key. Also, on the main toolbar, click on the "Views" tab. On the dropdown list, choose the "Viewport Configuration" option. In the "Viewport Configuration" dialog; open the "Statistics" tab. Enable the "Triangle Count" and the "Total" function, followed by "OK" to close it.

Viewport Configuration dialog

The selected viewport should now have the scene's statistics displaying the number of triangles, polys, etc.

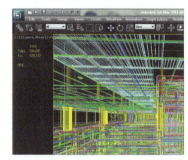

Scene Statistics

Once all the geometry is added; professionals often cache the geometry to speed up the rendering process.

When working in extremely complex exterior scenes with millions of triangles, the computer may crash at times.

To help override this, one should enable the "Use Fast Rasterizer (rapid motion blur)".This function may help overcome geometry issues, especially when working on exterior scenes.

It's worth mentioning that, this function although powerful, it disables the render elements.

In order to include the render elements, one is required to set the render output as an exr. file , and enable the relevant rendering passes.

Use Fast Rasterizer (Rapid Motion Blur) Enabled

If the scene has numerous reflective/refractive elements, it's common practice to reduce the global reflective/refractive values with caution (i.e. test render each value changed, to prevent artifacts).

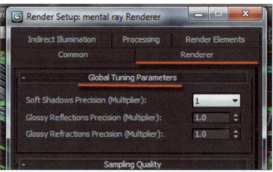

The global shadows and glossy precision should only be tweaked when necessary. Increasing these values will subsequently increase the rendering times slightly.

Reflections/Refractions   *Global Tuning Parameters*

When test rendering, it's strongly advised to reduce the sampling quality to draft.

This is mainly to speed up the test rendering process. One should only increase the sampling quality when fine-tuning final region/crop renders, and when sending the final render.

When the computer is struggling to cope with excessive amounts of geometry being generated from displacement materials, one should simply reduce the default value of Global "Max. Subdiv:" to 1k or less.

With GI and Final gather settings; prior to begin test rendering high resolution images (i.e. regions/crops), it's important to cache the solution at a lower output size (i.e. 500x... pixels); freeze and re-use the solution, at a higher resolution (i.e. 4000x... pixels).

With the solution frozen and set to be re-used, one can also increase the global image "Sampling Quality".

It's also worth carrying out basic overall test renders such as render elements (i.e. passes); etc.

Some of the most popular render passes used by professionals are:

Zdepth; Object IDs; Reflections and the Ambient Occlusion (AO).

Shadows & Displacement

As "Render Elements" increase the rendering times, production companies often render the passes in a separate scene, with an override material to compute the AO more accurately.

However, some render elements such as Material ID; Object ID, Diffuse, Reflection, etc, have to be processed in the main file.

1.20 Final Render Size:

Marketing images are often required to be rendered at high resolution (4000x…pixels or higher).
This is mainly to prevent common image artifacts such as grain, blur, jagged edges, etc.
Even some HD animations, are rendered at higher resolutions to prevent the above mentioned artifacts, especially when rendering interiors.
With HD animations, the high resolution frames would be later resized to an HD size; without affecting the overall quality.

1.21 Post work

The Post-production process is arguably the most important stage towards signing off the project.
All previous stages and technical decisions will culminate into this final phase.
Effects such as vignetting, depth of field, glow/glare, grain, colour correction, etc, are often applied and tweaked in post.

This is mainly to increase the work efficiency; ease of use and the flexibility that these effects can be added, tweaked or omitted in post.
In addition, such effects are often under more scrutiny by clients.
Because of this, when making vital technical decisions, it's imperative to facilitate the transition between rendering and post production.
Some of key technical points to consider when outputting frames are:

Render Elements/Passes

Due to time/budget constraints, and to give the client more flexibility to change numerous aspects of the final image output, it's good practise to enable key render passes such as object ID; Matte(i.e. multiple matte elements on the list); ZDepth; AO; Direct illumination; Indirect illumination; Material ID; Diffuse; Reflections; Self Illumination; Velocity; etc.
These rendered elements will enable the artist and the client to quickly address last minute changes, with help of powerful post-production tools such as: Curves; Hue/ Saturation; Masks; Levels; Glow; Blur; Photo Filter; etc.

Adding People

More often than not, clients may require their marketing images to be populated.

People often help "bring an image to live", and tell a story, by having individuals interact with the space.

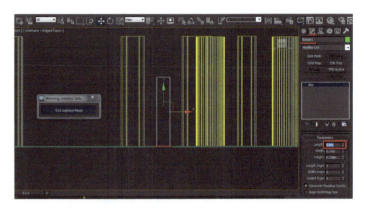
Dummy Box for Height reference

Assuming that the camera is at a correct height; professionals often create dummy objects/boxes as references, with self-illuminated colours representing their heights in the scene (1.60/1.75 m). These can be later rendered, separately, and fitted in post.

While in the main scene, ensure to have the dummy boxes' "Renderable" function disabled prior to rendering the main image.

Renderable option Disabled

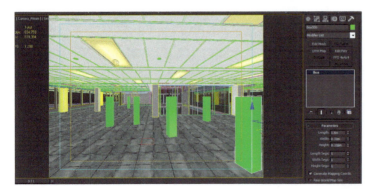
Dummy Boxes in the scene

Alternatively, one can simply use a screen grab of the relevant camera viewport, and resize it to fit proportially with the final output rendered image, in post.
Note that, the dummy objects are being used solely as height references, whilst adding real people in the shot

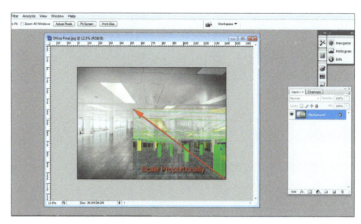

Scaling Proportionally the Screen Grab in Photoshop

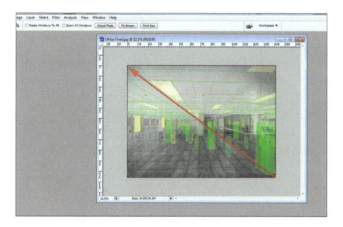

Fitting the Screen Grab Proportionally in Photoshop

Office Rendering: close up

Chapter 2
Production

Shading , Texturing & Lighting

2.1 Introduction

Having gone through the pre-production process and considered some of the technical approaches discussed earlier, it's now time to begin applying the shaders and textures to the final 3d shot. This chapter will take users through the intricacies of creating shaders and applying textures to surfaces. Most of the shaders created will be based on photo references sourced during the pre-production stage.

2.2 Units Setup

First, ensure to have the units set-up to "Metric", as opposed to default "generic units".

The metric unit scale can be either in millimeters, meters, centimeters, etc.
It's also essential to have the system unit scale set to "Respect System Units in Files".

Units Setup dialog

Open Max file

These precautionary measures will insure that incoming files are not accidently scaled.
When changed, simply click "OK" to exit the dialog box.

2.3 Setting up the Scene

1. Start by opening the file under the name of "Office_Floor_Start.max".

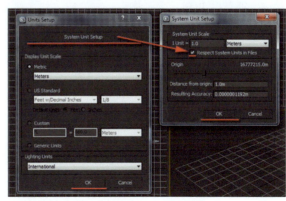

System Unit Setup dialog

2. If there are a units mismatch with the file, always choose to "Adopt the Files' Unit Scale". This function ensures that the original scale of the incoming file is kept.

3. The file should load up.
This scene is a typical commercial architectural interior office. Whereby the client often wants to sell the office space to potential clients (i.e. companies). At first glance, the scene appears to be straightforward. However, scenes such as this are renowned for being the most challenging, as extra attention

has to be paid to the overall lighting and finishes, to compensate for the lack of contents in the scene. By default, the Hardware Shading function is enabled, along with the ambient Occlusion.

For this exercise it wouldn't be beneficial to have these functions enabled. To disable it, simply left click on the "Ambient Occlusion + HW" text situated on the top left part of the viewport.

On the dropdown menu list, choose the "Lighting and Shadows" option, and click on the "Enable Hardware Shading" function, to disable it.

As planned, we will start by applying basic shaders and their respective textures, to all key objects in the scene. Once the lights are setup, we can then fine-tune key settings /parameters.

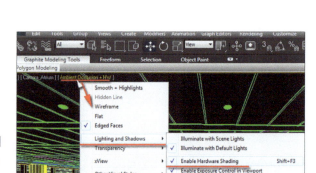

Units Mismatch dialog

Enable Hardware Shading function

4. To begin, we're going to load the mental ray renderer first.

5. Open the "Render Setup" dialog (f10).

6. In the "Common" tab; scroll down to the "Assign Renderer" rollout.

7. Open the rollout, and click on its "Production" toggle, followed by choosing the "mental ray renderer" from the list of "Choose Renderer" dialog.

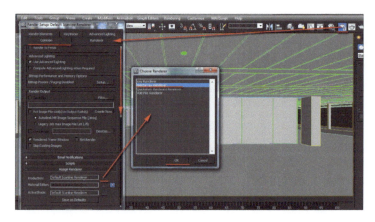

Choose Renderer dialog

8. It's also important to enable the gamma correction and the exposure settings.
On the main toolbar, click on the "Rendering" tab; followed by choosing the "Environment" option, from the dropdown list. Alternatively, simply press the "8" key shortcut.

Note that, if the key shortcut is not working, simply left click on any empty space of the main toolbar, followed by entering your key shortcut again.

9. In the "mr Photographic Exposure Control" rollout, under the "Physical Scale" group, choose the "Unitless" function. Increase its default value to 120000. This value should be high enough for most environment maps. Also, click on the "Setup" toggle to check the Gamma settings. Its default settings should be adequate for most scenes.

10. In the "Exposure Control" rollout, pick the "mr Photographic Exposure Control" from the list, and enable the "Process Background and Environment Maps" function. The "Process Background and Environment Maps" function will prevent a number of environment related artifacts from occurring in the render.

2.4 Creating the First Material: Glass

In this step, we will apply a glass material to all relevant objects in the scene, based on the photo reference.
Open the material editor (M) and select an empty slot. In the scene, select the object under the name of "_glass-a_atrium", and assign the selected slot to it.

Environment option

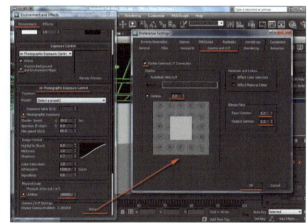
Environment and Effects with Preferences Settings dialog

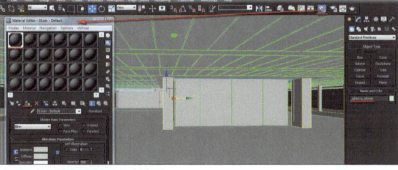
Assigning Material to an Object

1. Load up the "Arch & Design" shader by first clicking on the "standard" toggle to open the "material/map browser" dialog.

34

Material/Map Browser dialog

Open the "mental ray" rollout from the list; choose the "Arch & Design" shader and click "OK", to close the dialog box. The "Arch & Design" shader should now be loaded.

2. As mentioned earlier, it's important to have the photo references of the materials that the client had agreed to use.

It is common practice to load up the image/s in Max.

To do this, simply open the "Rendering" tab from the main toolbar. On the dropdown list, choose the "View Image File", followed by locating and picking the relevant file.

View Image File option

3. With the "Arch & Design" shader loaded, the next step is to choose the glass pre-set template, and tweak it to match with the photo reference.

Mental ray has a number glass pre-sets for a variety of purposes (i.e. goblets; thin glass; etc.). The one with physical attributes closer to the photo reference, is the "Glass (Thin Geometry)".

The "Glass (Thin Geometry)" physical properties are similar to the standard glass windows often found in most office buildings.

Choose the "Glass (Thin Geometry)" from the templates' dropdown list.

Test render to see the results (Shift+Q).

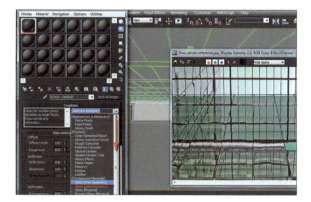

Material Templates List

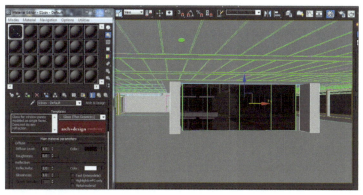

Glass (thin Geometry) pre-set

Glass (thin Geometry) Test render

4. The "Glass (Thin Geometry)" parameters are self-explanatory, especially when hovering over its buttons and functions.
By default, the glass colour is blue.

The next step is to closely match it with the photo reference.

5. Scroll down to the "Retraction" group.

6. Click on its "Color" swatch to bring up the "Color Selector" dialog box.

7. Click on the "Sample Screen Colour" button, followed by left clicking on the upper part of the photo reference displayed in Max. The RGB values of the "Color Selector" dialog should automatically change.

Also, name this shader according to the material template chosen (i.e. glass(thin Geometry)).

Color Selection dialog

8. As with most rendering engines, certain shader parameters are set too high, or too low by default. The next step is to quickly ensure that key parameters are set appropriately, to prevent extensive rendering times or artifacts.

9. One of the first parameters to change is the glossy interpolation. Pan down to the "Fast Glossy Interpolation" rollout and choose the "Interpolation Grid Density" of "1(same as rendering)" from the dropdown list. The default setting of "1/2 (half resolution)" is too low, and would have yielded glossy artifacts on glossy materials.

10. When using transparent materials for editing in post-production, it's always recommended to enable the "Transparency propagates Alpha channel" function. This function will help control the prominence of the glass reflection in post. To enable it, simply pan down to the "Advanced Rendering Options" rollout, in the "Advanced Transparency Options" group, turn on the above mentioned function.

Changing key Parameters

2.5 Creating the Second Material: Walls & Columns

Normally, professionals would take photos of walls/columns and map them directly onto the relevant 3d objects. However, since these objects are far away from the camera, and for the purpose of this exercise, we are only using a plain white material.

1. Select another empty material slot and assign it to the object under the name of "_column-covers-13".
Apply the "Arch & Design" shader to it" as previously done, and change its colour to white.

Color Selector dialog

2. The next step is to change the current material template to "Pearl Finish" by choosing it from the dropdown list. This material template is widely used as the basis to emulate most materials.

3. Rename this material as "Column covers (pearl Finish)", and disable the "Fast (interpolate)" function. This function is turned on by default to speed up the rendering process of glossy reflections and refractions.
However, it would have subsequently created glossy artifacts when rendering the final image.

It's prudent to have it turned off at all times, as a precautionary measure.
Also, to feather the glossy highlights and reflections, reduce the "Reflectivity" value to 0.3, and the "Glossiness" to 0.2. You may also try different values to see what works best.

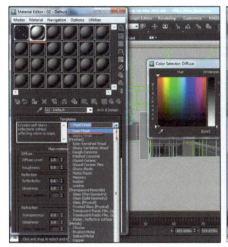

Pearl Finish Pre-set

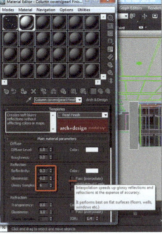

Changing key Parameters

4. Note in the material editor slot, how the glossy highlight is slightly diffused now. Also, change the "Glossy Samples" value to 6, to reduce the rendering times.

Changing Parameters and Isolating the object

5. Next, scroll down to the "Special Effects" rollout, and enable the "Round Corners" function.

As mentioned earlier, to preview the result of the "Fillet Radius" values without having to constantly test render; one should first isolate the column. Create a "Chamferbox" geometry with similar proportions to the column and tweak with its values in the viewport to see what works best.

The value of 10mm seemed ok. However, one can try different values, for different results.

Dummy ChamferBox Fillet Radius

2.6 Creating the Third Material: Floor

For this project, the client wanted to keep the existing floor material with specific tile dimensions (i.e. 433x433mm).

The floor sample was obtained by taking photos of the relevant floor, and by doing some work in Photoshop to ensure that most tiles looked different.

1. As previously done, we are going to create a "Perl Finish" material template and name it accordingly. Followed by sourcing the relevant texture- "floor colour 3"-, and assigning it to the floor object (i.e." _floor-offices").

2. In the "Bitmap Coordinates" decrease the "Blur" value to 0.01, to sharpen the appearance of the texture. Please note that this action may increase the rendering time…slightly.

Name Material and Open Material/Map Browser dialog

Pick the Floor Texture

3. Since the client had already chosen the floor texture material, our main focus will be to match its physical properties with the reference photos.

At this preliminary stage, we should simply add basic values, and leave the final tweaks to the very end, after the lights and most global parameters had been fine-tuned. This is the process used by most reputable CG companies:

Blur value 0.01

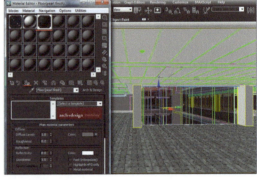

Assigning Material

4. As a starting point, we are going to set the reflectivity to 0.5; and the glossiness to 0.6 in the "Reflection" group. Note in the material editor slot, how the glossy highlight is slightly diffused now.
This will also have a direct impact on the reflection appearance.

5. Pan down to the "BRDF" rollout and increase the "0 deg. Refl:" value to 0.3 to start with. This parameter will increase the overall reflectivity slightly.
Also, change the interpolation grid density to "1(same as rendering)".

Changing the Reflection Parameters

Changing BRDF Parameters

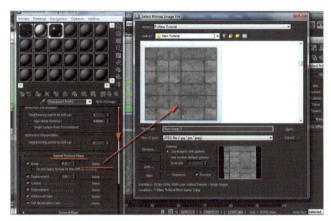

Applying the Bump Texture

As mentioned earlier, all these values will be fine-tuned at a later stage if necessary.

6. Next, we are going to apply a bump texture under the name of "floor bump 3" previously created.

7. Once the diffuse texture and the bump material had been applied, we should focus our attention in correcting the floor tiling.

8. As mentioned earlier, it has been determined that the floor tile would be 433x433mm. So the first thing to do is to select the floor object and isolate it.

9. Next, quickly create a rectangle with the above mentioned dimensions, in the top viewport.

Creating a Rectangle shape

10. Select the newly created rectangle in the front viewport, and move it up, so it sits above all floors (i.e. Z: 20718.989mm). This is to ensure that the rectangle shape is always visible, and on top of the floor texture.

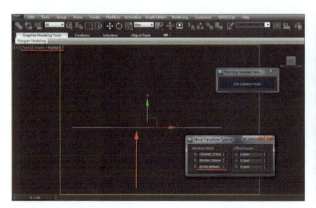

Moving up the Rectangle

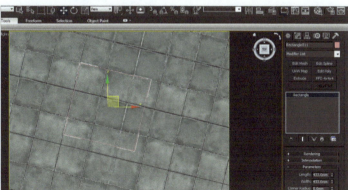

Rectangle on top of the Surface

11. To begin matching the tile size with the specified rectangle shape, we are going to first apply a simple "UVW Map" modifier from the "Modifier" command panel dropdown list.

12. Choose the "Box" mapping type parameters. In the "Material Editor" dialog, open its bitmap "Coordinates" parameters.

13. Move and change its "Offset" & "Tiling" values to fit the dimensions of the rectangle shape. For this exercise we have ended up with the following values: Offsett-U:-0.48; V:-0.09; Tiling-U:0.38; V:-0.4.

14. Also, copy and paste these values into the bump parameters once the UVW coordinates are set. Some artists find it easier to first copy the entire texture component from the diffuse toggle. Past it into the bump toggle; followed by replacing the texture thereafter.

Applying the UVW Map   Box Mapping type
Modifier

Changing Bitmap Coordinates

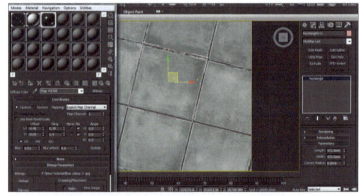

Adjusting the Texture to Fit the Rectangle Dimensions

15. Also, select and assign this texture to the surface under the name of "floor extra003".

To enable this new surface to acquire to the UVW map coordinates of the main floor, simply apply the "UVW Map" modifier first; followed by clicking on the "Acquire" button, and selecting the main floor surface, in the "Alignment" modifier group .

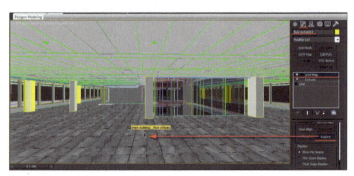

Acquire Alignment

The "Acquire UVW Mapping" dialog should pop up. Choose the "Acquire Absolute" option, followed by clicking "OK" to close the dialog. The texture parameters of both surfaces should now match seemingly and continuously.

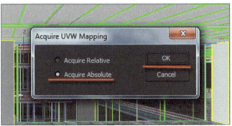

Acquire Absolute function

Both textures matching seemingly

2.7 Creating the Fourth Material: Metal Frames

As previously planned, prior to begin working on any material, one needs to source its photo reference first.

1. Open the photo reference under the name of "office ceiling detail photo reference2".

Note in photo how the metallic gloss is diffused throughout the greyish surface.

2. To emulate this physical property we are going to first choose an empty material slot in the material editor, and apply the "Arch & Design" shader to it.

View Image File option

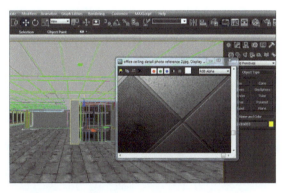

Office Ceiling Detail Photo Reference

Ceiling Metal Frame Selected

Also, select in the scene, the ceiling metal frame object under the name of "Metal Panel Frame02", and assign this new material slot to it.

42

3. Next, choose the "Brushed Metal" template from the "Arch & Design" material template list. This material template will help match the photo reference more closely.
Its core physical properties are briefly described on its template text field.

Also, re-name this material accordingly (i.e. Metal frame(brushed metal)).

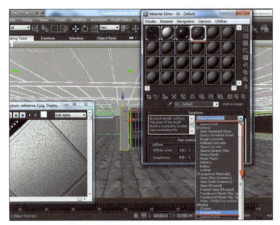
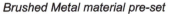

Brushed Metal material pre-set

Renaming the Material

4. As mentioned earlier, for the time being we are only applying the shaders and changing its main parameters. However, you may occasionally test render, mainly to check bitmap alignment/tiling; etc.
Since there are no lights or GI, the renders should be fairly quick!

Also, change the "Metal (brushed metal)" interpolation grid density to "1(same as rendering)" and apply a basic UVW map modifier to it.

2.8 Creating the Fifth Material: Ceiling Panel

1. Pick the ceiling panel in the scene, under the name of "_ceiling-metal3". Choose another empty material slot and load the "Arch & Design" shader. For this ceiling panel material we are going to start by applying a simple "Pearl Finish" template and assigning it to the relevant object.

Pearl Finish Material for Ceiling Panel

2. It's worth mentioning that the client had also supplied the ceiling texture, and instructed that the ceiling had to be slightly reflective. In the diffuse toggle, use the texture under the name of "ceiling bump" and enable the "Use Real-World Scale" function in the bitmap "Coordinates".

3. Also, click on the "Show Standard Map in view" button. These functions will be quite useful to control the appearance of the tiny ceiling grains. In addition, apply the "UVW Mapping" modifier; followed by choosing the "Box" mapping type and enabling the "Real-World Map Size".

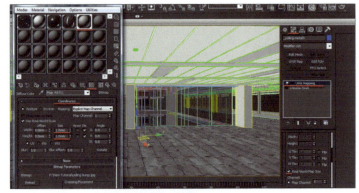

Changing Bitmap Coordinates

Picking the Ceiling Texture

The grain size on the surface doesn't look correct, when compared with the photo reference previously loaded in Max.

4. Back in the bitmap parameters of the material editor, change the size value from 100m to 1.0m.

Note how the ceiling grain and its size are evenly spread across the surface now. It's often useful to "play" around with these values to see what works best.

5. Back in the "Main Material Parameters", re-name this material accordingly (i.e. ceiling metal (pearl finish)) and uncheck the "Fast (interpolate)" function.

To add a bit of shine to the shader, simply change its reflectivity value to about 0.4 and the glossiness to about 0.5. The shader now displays a slight shine to it.

The glossiness of most office ceiling panels are considerably spread across, as opposed to concentrated.

6. To emulate this effect, simply pan down to the "BRDF" parameters and increase the "0 deg. Refl:" to about 0.7.

Note in the mateial editor slot, how the glossy highlight looks more diffused now. Also, change the interpolation grid

Changing the Reflection values

Changing the BRDF values

density to "1 (same as rendering)". It's very important not to waste time test rendering the glossy results at this early stage.

Most materials will require further tweaks once the lights and the global parameters have been fine-tuned.

2.9 Creating the Sixth Material: Ceiling Lights

1. Select a new empty slot in the material editor, and load the "Arch & Design" shader.

View Image file   *Renaming the Material*

2. Assign it to the respective object and apply the "Pearl Finish" material template to it. Followed by naming it accordingly (i.e. Light fitting (pearl finish).

3. Next, we are going to bring into Max, the photo reference of this light.

Note in the photo, the intensity of the lights and the slight yellow rim around the edges. While we could easily emulate this effect in Max, it's often best to do it in post.
The reason being is that, overexposed pixels are very difficult to tweak in post, due to lack of information or data retained in these affected areas (i.e. overexposed areas).

2. We are going to start by unchecking the "Fast (interpolate)" function, and changing the interpolation grid density to "1 (same as rendering)".

3. To emulate the intensity of a lit light, we are going to pan down to the "Self-Illumination (Glow)" rollout parameters, and enable the "Self Illumination (Glow)" function.

Disabling the Fast (interpolate) function

In the "Luminance" group, enable the "Physical Units: (cd/m2)" function. This luminance option will prevent artifacts related to glossy reflections on other surfaces. The default value of 1500 is often not high enough to produce a bright effect. Change it to 12000.0 for now. And keep the "Glow Options" to be "Visible in Reflections" only.

4. Next, we are going to apply a realistic texture (i.e. photo) of a similar ceiling light.

Click on the filter toggle and use the texture under the name of "uplight_03_w copy".

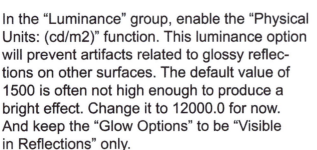

Degrees Kelvin	Type of Light Source	Indoor (3200k) Color Balance	Outdoor (5500k) Color Balance
1700-1800K	Match Flame		
1850-1930K	Candle Flame		
2000-3000K	Sun: At Sunrise or Sunset		
2500-2900K	Household Tungsten Bulbs		
3000K	Tungsten lamp 500W-1k		
3200-3500K	Quartz Lights		
3200-7500K	Fluorescent Lights		
3275K	Tungsten Lamp 2k		
3380K	Tungsten Lamp 5k, 10k		
5000-5400K	Sun: Direct at Noon		
5500-6500K	Daylight (Sun + Sky)		
5500-6500K	Sun: through clouds/haze		
6000-7500K	Sky: Overcast		
6500K	RGB Monitor (White Pt.)		
7000-8000K	Outdoor Shade Areas		
8000-10000K	Sky: Partly Cloudy		

Kelvin Colour Temperature values chart

Since this material will be self-illuminated, one should decrease all its "Reflection" values to 0.0. Also, enable the "Show Standard Map in Viewport" function, to view the texture.

7. Apply the "UVW Map" modifier to the object, and choose the "Box" mapping type.

8. Click again on the "UVW Mapping" modifier to enable its gizmo display in the viewport. The gizmo and the texture don't seem to line up with the geometry.

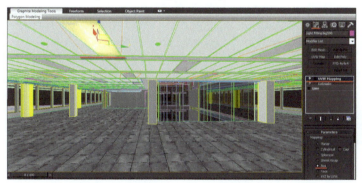

UVW Map Gizmo not Aligning

If not familiar with "kelvin" colour temperature values, simply check its standard chart.

5. We are also going to use the same texture in its diffuse colour.

First, copy this texture from the glow "Filter" toggle by right clicking on it and choosing to "Copy" it from the pop up list.

6. Next, pan up to the "Main Material Parameters"; and paste instance this texture into its "Color" toggle.

Copy Texture toggle

Paste (Instance) Texture toggle

Show Standard Map in Viewport

9. To fix this we are going to start by isolating the object first.

10. In the top the viewport, right click and choose to "Rotate" the gizmo.
Rotate the gizmo until it lines up with the object's shape; followed by clicking the ""Fit" button in the modifier's "Alignment" group.

The gizmo and the texture should now fit perfectly. If not, align it further by rotating it and clicking the "Fit" button again.

Rotate tool

Rotating the Gizmo

11. Once finished, exit the isolation mode, and switch to the camera viewport. Apply this texture to all the relevant objects in the scene.

2.10 Creating the Seventh Material: Fire Detector

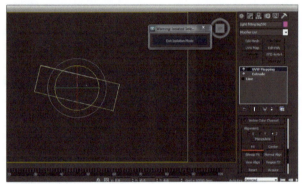

Fit Alignment

1. Select in the scene, the object under the name of "fire detector". For this material we are going to apply a simple white "Pearl Finish" material template, with a slight shine to it. Further adjustments will be made once the lights have been added.

Changing the Fast Glossy Interpolation

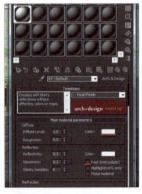

Disabling the Fast (interpolate)

2. Also, ensure to disable the "Fast (interpolate)" function; followed by changing the interpolation grid density to "1 (same as rendering)" and renaming this new material (i.e. fire detector (pearl finish).

Apply this texture to all the relevant objects in the scene.

2.11 Creating the Daylight System

1. To quickly begin setting up the lights, we are going to temporarily override the textures and its shaders first.

2. Open the "Render Setup" dialog by pressing the "F10" key.

3. Select the "Processing" tab rollout; under the "Material Override" group turn on the "enable" function.

4. Open the material editor (M), and create a basic white "Arch & Design" shader, without reflections.

5. Drag & drop this newly created material into the "Material Override" toggle. A dialog should pop up; choose the "Instance" copy method and click "OK". All changes made to this material in the material editor will now have a direct impact in the "Material Override" parameters.

Copy Instance Method

6. Press the "Shift+Q" keys to test render the results. This first render result may look slightly too bright. To rectify this, simply change the "Main Material Parameters" colour to a darker tone, by simply clicking on its colour swatch and sliding up the "Color Selector: Diffuse" arrow a little bit.

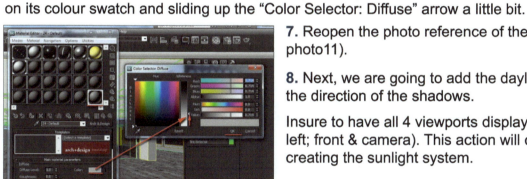

Color Selector: Diffuse dialog

7. Reopen the photo reference of the office space (i.e. photo11).

8. Next, we are going to add the daylight object, and set the direction of the shadows.

Insure to have all 4 viewports displayed in Max (i.e. top; left; front & camera). This action will come handy when creating the sunlight system.

9. In the main toolbar, click on the "Create" tab.

10. On the dropdown list, go to "Lights" and choose the "Daylight System" option.

11. A target (+) cursor should appear. In the top viewport, left click, hold and drag the cursor to create the daylight compass first.
Once satisfied with its size; release the left click button to resume the compass creation and continue dragging the mouse to create the daylight system object.

Left click to finish creation once the daylight object is created and right click thereafter to completely exit the creation.

The 4 viewports should help control the height of the daylight system object.

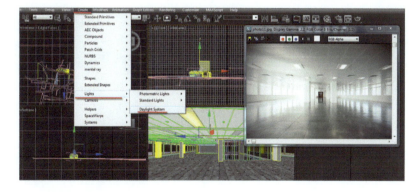

Daylight System creation

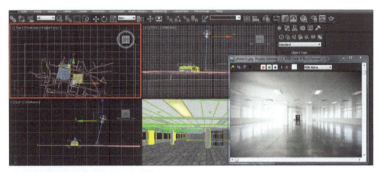

End Daylight System creation

Changing to mr Sun type

2.12 Positioning the Daylight System

1. While the daylight object is still selected, open the modify command panel and pan down to the "Daylight Parameters" rollout.

2. Change the sunlight type to "mr sun"; and the skylight to "mr Sky".

mental ray Sky dialog

3. The "mental ray sky" dialog should pop up; click "yes" to accept the automatic creation of "mr Physical sky" environment map.

4. The next task is to make the sunlight shadows fall inside the office and close to the left windows (i.e. in a similar position to the photo reference).

5. Before beginning to manually move the daylight object, enable the "Manual" function first, in the "Position" group.

6. With the "Move" toolbar, begin repositioning the daylight object to match the shadow direction depicted in the photo reference. If you possess a good graphics card, simply turn on again the "Enable Hardware Shading" function. This function will help you control the direction of the shadows in the viewport, in real time.

7. Otherwise, simply carry out some quick test renders to see where the sunlight shadows are falling. The test renders should not take longer than 12 seconds, at this stage.

8. The daylight X Y Z position should be as follows: X= -289400.881mm

Y= 54792.878mm; Z= 246391.023mm

Also, feel free to try different position values. *Positioning the Daylight Object*

Test rendering of the Daylight position

Also note that, if you find that millimeter display values are unmanageable, simply change the "display unit Scale" to meters instead.

Professionals often switch between "Display Unit Scale" value types depending on the level of detail they're working on. This specific function only affects the unit values being displayed. Not the physical scale of the objects.

2.13 Daylight System Settings

At first glance, the horizon line of the environment seems too high in the rendered dialog.

1. Open the daylight modify parameters.

2. In the "-mr Sky Advanced Parameters" rollout decrease the horizon height to about -5.0 or lower.

3. Prior to test rendering the results, open the render setup dialog (F10). In the "Common" tab, lock the "Image Aspect..." and the "Pixel Aspect". This will ensure that the image output size will always be in proportion, when increased or decreased.

Fine-tuning the mr Sky Horizon Height, and the Output Size

Also, lock the camera "View", to avoid rendering other viewports accidentally. Press the "Shif+Q" keys, to test render the results.

4. Now that the skyline is corrected, we are going to increase the sky brightness, to closely match the photo reference. As mentioned earlier, it's prudent not to "scorch" textures directly in Max; as it will be difficult/impossible to fine-tune in Post.

5. Open the "Environment and Effects" dialog by pressing the "8" key. Note that, if the key shortcut is not working, simply left click on any empty space of the main toolbar, followed by pressing the the "8" key again.

6. Next, open the material editor (m). In the "Environment Map" toggle, drag and drop the "(mr Physical sky)" component into an empty slot of the material editor. Accept the "Instance" copy "Method".

Copy Instance mr Physical Sky

7. The "mr physical sky" parameters should now be visible in the material editor slot.

Note that, by default these parameters are directly linked to the sky object in the scene. To edit the sky environment without any direct impact in the global illumination, simply uncheck the "Inherit from mr Sky" function.

Also, match the "Horizon Height" value with the sky object (i.e. -5.0) and increase the multiplier to about 1.8. Test render the changes (Shift+Q).

Test rendering the mr Sky changes

One can try different multiplier values if desired.

8. The sky environment seems much brighter now.
Next, we are going to increase the brightness of the overall scene and the sky environment slightly.

Changing the mr Physical Sky Parameters

9. In the "mr Photographic Exposure Control" rollout, reduce the "Shutter Speed" value to about 30.0 and test render.

10. The sky environment and the window areas seem much brighter now. However, the bright spots don't seem to be balanced. Decrease the "Aperture (f-stop):" value to 8.0 and the "Film Speed (ISO):" to about 60.0. You can tweak with different values if desired.

Shutter Speed value of 30.0

Aperture and Film speed values changed

2.14 Fine-Tuning the Final Gather & Adding Artificial Lights

1. Open the "Render Setup" dialog (F10).

2. In the "Indirect Illumination" tab, increase the "Rays per FG point" value to 200. This function increases the number of final gather rays emitted in the scene. Higher values will result in more light bounces. It may also increase fg calculation times slightly.

3. Also, increase the "Diffuse Bounces" to 1. Note that, values higher than 1 may result in a drastic increase of rendering times. Test render the changes (Shift+Q).

4. So far, the rendering times have been reasonably low (i.e. 32 seconds). The next step is to begin adding artificial lights in the scene.

5. Select the top viewport.

6. In the "Create" panel tab; click on the "Lights" command, and choose the "Free Light" type, by clicking, and placing it in the scene (i.e. left click to drop it, followed by right clicking to exit creation).

7. In "Front" viewport, select the newly created light and move it close to the top most ceiling light object. It's exact X Y Z position should be: X=-143604.997mm

Y= 298318.453mm

Z=19973.372mm

Final Gather Parameters changed

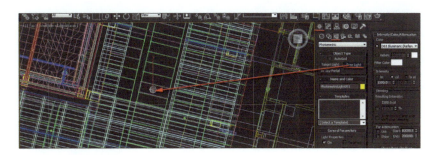

Creating a Free Light

52

8. In the light's modify "General Parameters", enable the "Shadows" and change the shadow type to "Ray Traced Shadows". Ray traced shadows work best with mental ray.

9. In the "Light Distribution Type", change it to "Uniform Diffuse". This type of light distribution is often best to emulate this light model.

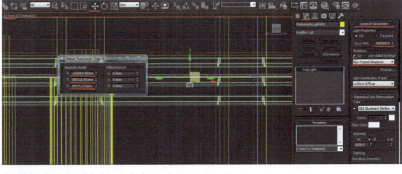

Positioning the Light and changing parameters

10. To ensure that the direction of the "Free Light" is downwards, professionals often turn on the "Targeted" function. In "Front" viewport, the light target dummy is selected and moved downwards towards the floor.

Once finished, the "Targeted" function is turned off again, to have more flexibility to move the lights in the viewport.

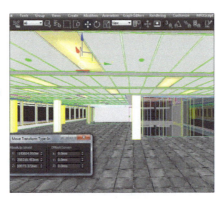

Correcting the Light position

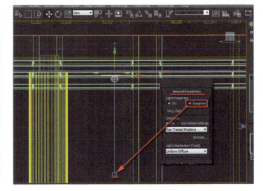

Changing the Light type to Target

11. To emulate the ceiling light model, we are going to change its current shape from "Point" to "Rectangle", in the "Shape/Area Shadows" rollout.

Also, in its "Rendering" group, we are going decrease the shadow samples to "16". The value of 32 should only be used when absolutely necessary, as it will increase the rendering times substantially.

Changing the light shape to Rectangle

12. As the light shape was changed to rect-angle, the shape didn't seem to have aligned correctly with the ceiling light model.

13. In the top viewport, change the type selec-tion filter to "Lights".

Changing the type of Selection Filter to Lights   *Selecting the Rotate tool*

This is to restrict the selection type to lights only, and avoid selecting other objects in the scene accidentally.

14. While the light is still selected, right click and choose the rotate tool from the pop up list.

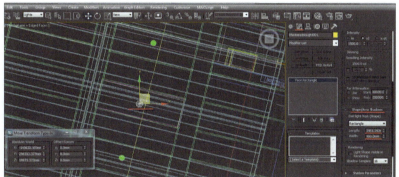

15. Rotate the light until it's completely aligned with the ceiling light object.

Also, resize its length and width values to make it fit (i.e. Length=1461.292mm ; Width=480.0mm), and move it further if necessary. Test render the results.

Rotating and changing the Light dimensions

16. The light doesn't seem to cause a major impact in the scene.

Next, we are going to increase its multiplier values, and copy lights across the scene. As discussed earlier, lights are only added in strategic areas of the scene.

This "trick" is to help decrease the rendering times dramatically whilst trying to emulate as if all lights in the scene are turned on.

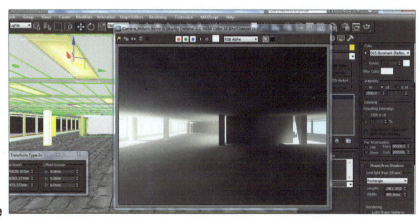

Test Rendering the Light changes

17. In the light's "Dimming" group parameters , enable the "Resulting Intensity" function and increase it to 2.000. Test render the results.

18. The light intensity results are more visible in the render now. In top viewport, copy instance this light, and move it close to the next ceiling light model. Adjust its position to align correctly. Test render again, to see the results.

Increasing the Resulting Intensity

Also note in the render how the shadows are nicely diffused. This is mainly to do with the dimension of the light rectangle: Bigger dimensions will result in softer shadows.

Copying Lights

Test Rendering the Results

Test rendering each light created is a good practise to prevent the scene from "bleaching out" suddenly, when adding too many lights and/or for not positioning the lights far enough from each other.

Most importantly, there has to be a clear definition between bright and dark areas in scene, in order to create depth (i.e. realism).

19. Create another 20 lights across the floor by repeating the previous steps (i.e. every light needs to be fairly distant from one another). The scene shouldn't take longer than 3 minutes to render; even with 22 lights in the scene.

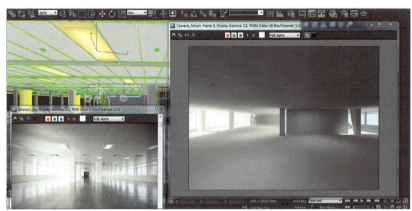

Creating 20 more Lights and Test Rendering the Results

2.15 Fine-Tuning Materials & Global Parameters

This final production stage will be dedicated to refining the materials, lights and the global parameters

1. Open the render setup dialog (F10) and disable the "Material Override" function, in the processing tab.

2. Test render (Shift+Q).

. When comparing the latest render against the photo reference:

. At first glance, the ceiling light geometry and the environment seem too bright.

. Also, the ceiling panels and the walls require brightening up a bit. In addition, the atrium glass colour could be toned down slightly.

3. Open the "Material Editor" dialog (M), and the "Environment and Effects "dialog (8).
In the "Environment" tab, under the "Image Control" group, decrease the "Highlights (Burn)" to 0.0.

This function will help reduce the amount of "overblown" areas in the scene.

Test Rendering the Results without Material Override

Decreasing the Highlights (Burn) value to 0.0; and the Glossy Samples to 6.0

4. Select the floor material from the material editor.In the "Main Material Parameters", change the "Roughness" to 0.0. This function will help smooth the surface. Also, in the "Reflection" group, decrease the "Glossy Samples" value to about 6. This will help reduce the rendering times, without affecting the quality much.

5. Pan down to the "Special Effects" rollout and enable the "Ambient Occlusion"; and set its "Max Distance" to about 2000.0mm. This value worked ok. However, you can try different values to see what works best.

The ambient occlusion will help "ground/connect" objects close to this surface.

6. Next, in the "Advanced Rendering Options" rollout, under the "Advanced Reflectivity Options" group, increase the "Relative Intensity of Highlights" to 2.5.
As previously discussed, glossy highlights contribute a great deal in making an image appealing. You may also try different values, and test render to see what works best for you.

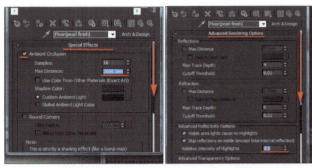

Setting the Ambient Occlusion value to 2000mm   Increasing Relative Intensity of Highlights value to 2.5

7. The next material to fine-tune is the wall. Select its material slot and enable the "Highlights+FG only" function, in the "Reflection" group. Enabling this function will help speed up the rendering times, by retaining the materials' glossiness without reflecting the environment .
Also, enable the "Ambient Occlusion" and set its "Max distance" to 2000.

Next, we are going to increase its brightness by first opening the "Advanced Rendering Options" rollout. In the "Indirect Illumination Options" group, increase the "FG/GI multiplier" to 2.0. This powerful function will help increase the brightness of indirectly lit areas of the object.

Enabling the Highlights+FG

Enabling the Ambient Occlusion

8. The ceiling panels also require brightening up a bit. Select its material and increase the "FG/GI multiplier" to about 5.0. In addition, enable the "Ambient Occlusion" function.

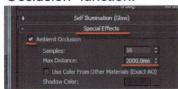

Increasing the FG/GI multiplier value to 5.0   Increasing the FG/GI multiplier value to 5.0   Increasing the FG/GI multiplier value to 2.0

9. Finally, change the current glass colour to light green...and test render the scene.

10. The overall lighting and "feel" of the render are now closer to the photo reference.
Use the previous steps to tweak further with the panel frames (i.e. too dark), back wall, fire detector, etc.

Changing the Glass colour

2.16 Saving the FG file

Before sending the final big render, we are going to save the Final Gather file and increase the image quality.

1. Open the "Render Setup" dialog (F10).

2. In the "Indirect Illumination" tab, increase the "Initial FG Point Density" to about 0.3. This function will add more depth (i.e. more darker areas=diffused shadows) to the scene by "shooting" more final gather points during the FG calculation process. It's worth noting that this may increase the FG processing time slightly. Higher values will produce better results.

Test rendering the Results

3. Next we are going to set mental ray to save the FG file prior to sending the final big render. Pan down to the "Reuse (Fg and GI Disk caching)" rollout, and enable the "Calculate FG/GI and Skip Rendering" function.

This function allows mental ray to compute and save the final gather only. It's often used after all test renders had been carried out.

4. Next, in the "Final Gather Map" group, choose the name and the location for the fg map file to be saved into, by clicking on its toggle.

5. Click render (Shift+Q) to save the fg map.

Decreasing the Initial FG Point Density to 0.3

Using the Reuse (FG and GI Disk Caching)

6. Once the FG process is completed (i.e. FG map automatically saved). In the "Final Gather Map" group, change the FG process type to "Read FG Points Only from Existing Map files".

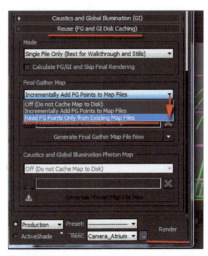

2.17 Fine-Tuning the Renderer Parameters

Next, we are going to increase the sampling quality of the final image.

1. Open the "Renderer" tab. In the "Sampling Quality" rollout, change the "Minimum" samples per pixel to 1; and the "Maximum" to 16. These are the standard values to achieve good image quality results. Higher "Maximum" values will result in longer rendering times.

Enabling Read FG Points Only from Existing Map Files

2. Change the filter type to "Mitchell". This filter type sharpens the render results. Followed by increasing its default "width" & "Height" value to 5.0.

Also, turn on the "Jitter" function. This function helps correct jagged pixels.

3. In the "Rendering Algorithms" rollout, under the "Reflections/Refractions" group, reduce the "Max. Trace Depth" to 3. This will help speed up the rendering times.

4. Change the "Max. Reflections" value to 3. This value should also help reduce the rendering times, without causing artifacts.

5. Also, decrease the "Max.Refractions" value to 3.

Changing the Sampling Quality and enabling Jitter

Decreasing the Reflections/ Refractions parameters

2.18 Region Renders & Saving the Final Output File

1. As previously planned, we are going to send few region renders to look for possible artifacts.

2. In the "Common" tab, under the "Area to Render" group; change it to "Region" type.

3. In the "Output Size" group, change the "Width" to 4000. The "Height" value should change automatically as the pixel and image aspects are locked. This image size will ensure that the printing quality is very high.

4. In the camera viewport, choose a region to test render, by adjusting and moving its rectangular marquee.

5. When satisfied with the region test renders, simply change the "Area to Render" type to "View".
In the "Render Output" group, enable the "Save File" function, and name it. Choose the TGA file type; enable the "Pre-Multiplied Alpha" function to "32 bits per pixel" and turn on the "Compress" option.

This option will allow users to save the Alpha Channels for the environment and the reflections/refractions (i.e. the "transparency propagates alpha channel").

It's worth mentioning that a number of professionals also use EXR file extensions. However, due to its incompatibility with some versions of Photoshop, it's best to use TGA for this exercise.

6. It is now time to start adding render elements (i.e. passes).
When deciding to use render elements, it's worth remembering that certain elements such as "Material ID", "Object ID", "Reflections", "Specular", etc. need to be used in the main scene (not separately). Other elements such as the ambient occlusion and the Z Depth are often pro cessed in a separate Max file due to the amount of fine-tuning required.

2.19 Render Elements

Render elements may increase the rendering times slightly. This is typical with most rendering engines. In this exercise we are only using the object ID element. However, feel free to add other elements, if desired.

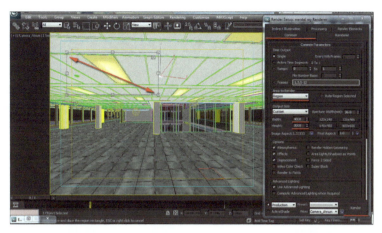

Region Rendering at full resolution

Renderer Output File dialog

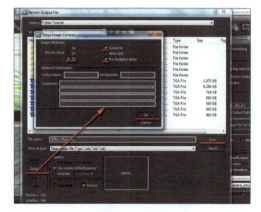

Setting up the Targa Image Control

To add object ID numbers, simply select an object in the scene; right click and choose the "Object Properties" option from the pop up list.

Under the "General Parameters" tab, simply type in a number in the "G-Buffer" group. Repeat this action by adding different numbers to different objects with different materials applied.

1. One may also add the "Material ID" render element in case the user wants to use different ID numbers for a variety of material channels/toggles (i.e. bump; diffuse; etc).

In the "Render Element" tab, add the "Object ID" by clicking on the "Add" toggle and choosing it from the "Render Element" dialog list.

Choosing the Object Properties option

Adding Object ID

2. Pan down and turn on the "Enable Filtering" function in the "Selected Element Parameters". This function will help smooth jagged pixels.

By default, 3Ds Max automatically names the render element according to the original render file name.

This is mainly to keep the elements' name coherent with the main render file name.
One can manually change it, if desired.

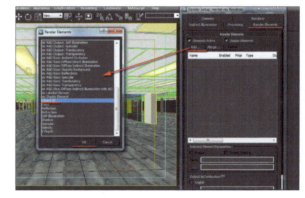

Render Elements dialog

Object ID Element

Send the final file to render.

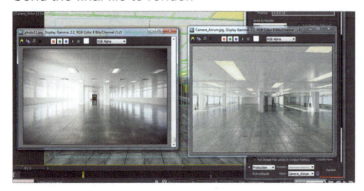

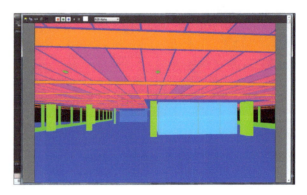

Final Render

Object ID element rendered

The next phase is to tweak the ambient occlusion and the Z Depth in a separate file.

3. Open the Max file under the name of "Office_Render Passes.max"

4. To quickly set-up the Ambient Occlusion as the basis to start rendering passes, go to the main toolbar and click on "Tools". On the dropdown list choose the "Light Lister" tool; and disable all the listed lights by unchecking them.

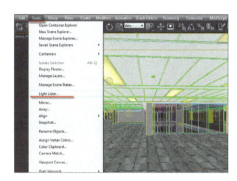

Light Lister tool

Enabling Material Override

5. Open the "Render Setup" dialog. In the "Processing" tab, enable the "Material Override" function.

Light Lister dialog

Loading mental ray Shader

6. Open the "Material Editor" dialog and select the "Material Override" slot. Replace the current "Arch & Design" shader with the "mental ray" shader, by selecting it from the "Material/Map browser" dialog list.

7. Once loaded, in "Material shaders" rollout, click the "Surface" toggle and choose the "Ambient/Reflective Occlusion" from the "Material/Map Browser" dialog list.

Loading Ambient/Reflective Occlusion shader

8. The next step is to open the "Environment and Effects" dialog. Turn off the environment "Exposure Control"; disable the "Environment Map"; change the "Background" and the "Ambient" colour swatch to white. This is to ensure that the scene is not overblown.

Changing the Ambient colour swatch

9. Open the "Render Setup" dialog. In the "Indirect Illumination" tab; under "Final Gather Map" group, switch to "Off (Do not Cache to Disk) option. This is to ensure that the FG is not reading from a saved file.

In the "Renderer" tab, under the "Sampling Quality", switch to draft mode (i.e. min samples per pixel= 1/4; maximum=4).

Also, change the "Filter" type to "Box". These changes will speed up the rendering times. Test render to see the results .

Enabling the Off (Do not Cache Map to Disk)

Changing the Sampling Quality

Test Rendering the Changes

10. The ambient occlusion is not as visible as expected. To make it more prominent simply increase the "Spread" to about 10.0. The "Spread" function sets the diameter of the ambient occlusion.

Also, increase the "Max Distance" value to about 1000mmm. This function sets the gradient radius of the ambient occlusion. Test render to see the results.

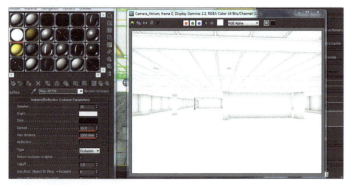

Changing the Spread and Max distance values

11. The ambient occlusion is more visible now. However, it seems a bit grainy. Increase the AO samples to 60, and test render again. The results are much smoother now.

Also bear in mind that when the image sampling quality is changed back to 1/16, and the filter type to "Mitchell", the results are going to be even smoother.

12. Now is the time to add the Z Depth element. In the "Render Setup" dialog, open the "Render Elements" tab and click on the "Add" toggle.
In the "Render Elements" dialog list, choose the "Z Depth".

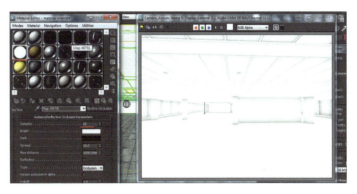

Test Rendering the AO Samples Results

Adding ZDepth Element

13. Test render to see the first results.
There's currently no contrast in the Z Depth render (i.e. completely white).

14. Pan down to the "Z Depth Element Parameters" rollout. Due to the "Display Unit Scale" being in millimeters, the Z Depth values may seem too long to manage.

Simply change the "Display Unit Scale" to meters.

15. To set the contrast of the Z Depth, we are going to change the " Z Min" value to 0.0m and the "Z Max" to 5.0m. Test render.

As mentioned earlier, the Z Depth works best with objects in the foreground.

Increase the "Z Max" value to 10.5m, and test render again.

The Z Depth contrast is looking much better now.

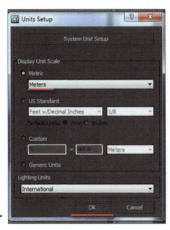

Changing the Display Unit Scale   Changing the Z Depth parameters

It's important to change key settings prior to sending the final render passes.

16. In the "Common" tab, increase the "Width" & "Height" Output Size to 4000x3000.

17. In the "Render Output" group, enable the "Save File" function.

18. In the "Renderer" tab, change the "Samples Per Pixel" to 1/16 and the filter to "Mitchell"...and send the Render.

Increasing the Output Size and Saving   *Changing the Sampling Quality*

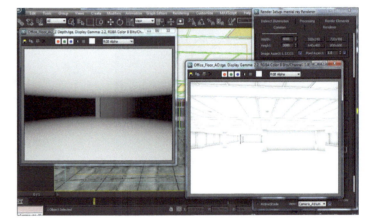

Final Render

Photo Reference & Office Rendering

Chapter 3
Post-Production

3.1 Introduction

The Post-production process is arguably the most important stage towards signing off a project. All previous stages and the technical decisions will culminate into this final process.

3.2 Vignetting

Effects such as vignetting, depth of field, glow/glare, grain, colour correction, etc., are often applied and tweaked in post. Mostly due to these effects being under more scrutiny by clients.

Applying these effects in post increases the work efficiency when matching the photo reference closely. It will also provide more flexibility to add or omit such effects if/when necessary.

In Photoshop, open the file under the name of "Office_Floor_Big". Also, open the Photo reference under the name of "photo11".

Photo Reference and Rendered image

The first effect from the photo reference to be emulated is the "vignetting". Note that this effect could have been easily created in Max. However, in real production environment it's best to add it in post, as it will give users the flexibility to quickly turn it "On" or "Off", instead of having to re-render the entire scene again...if the client decides to omit it.

1. In the side toolbar choose the "Elliptical Marquee Tool", by pressing and holding its icon.

2. Select the "Office_Floor_Big" document. Click, hold & drag the elliptical marquee tool from the bottom right corner of the document, to the top left corner. Release the mouse to exit creation.

The next step is to feather the selection.

3. In the main toolbar click the "Select"tab. On the dropdown list, choose "Modify", followed by selecting the "Feather" tool (Alt+Cttrl+D).

4. The "Feather Selection" dialog should pop up. Set the "Feather Radius" to 200 pixels. This value will ensure that pixel edges of the selection are very smooth. Also note that, depending on the document size, the results may differ. Only through trial & error one can determine the correct feather value for each document size.

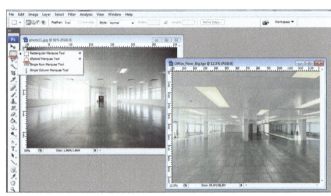

Choosing the Elliptical Marquee Tool

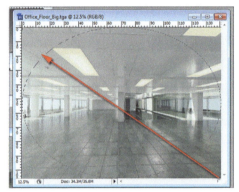

Creating the Elliptical Marquee Tool

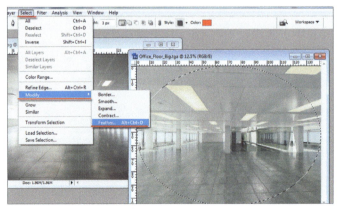

Feathering the edge selection

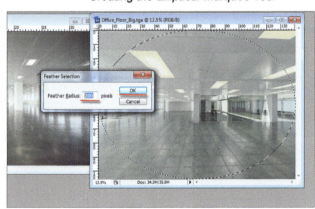

Setting the Feather Radius

Currently, the selection is at the centre of the document. The next step is to invert the selection, so the selected areas are around the boarders of the document.

5. Simply press "Shift+Ctrl+I" keys to invert the selection. Or simply click the "Select" tab and choose "Inverse" from the dropdown list.

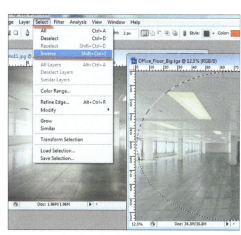

Inverse selection tool

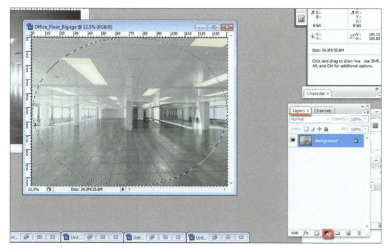

Selection Inverted

6. While the selection is still on; add an "Adjustment Layer", by clicking on its icon and choosing the "Levels" adjustment layer from the list.

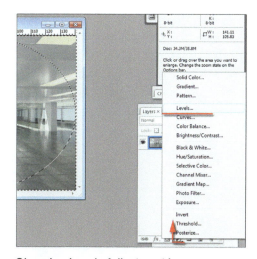

Choosing Levels Adjustment layer

7. In the "Levels" dialog simply drag the "Output Levels" slider to the left, to darken the selection. You can try different levels of darkness, if desired.
Adjustment layers are very useful to control the prominence of certain effects.

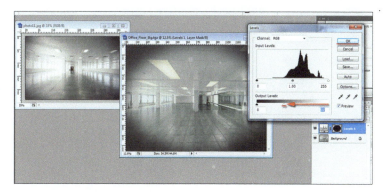

Decreasing the Output Levels

70

To closely match the shape and the appearance of the "vignetting" effect in the photo reference, we are going to use the brush tool in conjunction with the layer masks.

8. Select the "Brush Tool" (B) from the side tool bar, followed by adjusting its size, and clicking on the brush icon from the main toolbar.

9. Choose a very soft brush with feathered edges(68 pixels).

10. Increase the current brush size to about 1200, by simply pressing and holding down the "]" key.

Bigger brush sizes cover much bigger areas. To reduce its size simply press the "[" key. Also reduce the brush opacity to about 7%. This will help you have better control over the areas to mask out. The mask works best when the foreground/background colour swatches are black & white, in the side toolbar.

Selecting the Brush Tool

Selecting the Brush Preset picker

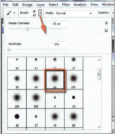
Selecting the Brush type

Brushing with the Vector mask tool

End result of Brushing with the Vector mask tool

Black omits areas of the selected layer and white does the opposite. Use the "X" key to switch between colours.

Foreground/Background Colour Switches

11. Begin brushing around the relevant areas of the "vignetting" layer, to match its shape and appearance with the photograph. You may also reduce its layer opacity, if required.

3.3 Curves

Next, we are going to brighten up the render slightly, to match the photo reference:

1. In the "Layers" tab, select the "Background" layer first.

2. Click the "Adjustment Layer" button, and choose the "Curves" adjustment layer from the list.

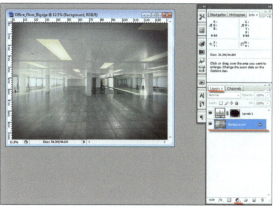

Selecting the Background Layer

Adding Curves adjustment layer

3. In the dialog, add a point by simply clicking on its spline with the cursor. Move the point up slightly towards the centre of the graph. Note the impact of this action in the document. Add another point in the lower part of the curve to balance the brightness.

4. In the curves' "Channel", choose "Red" from the dropdown list. Add a point in the middle and move it up slightly. See how the red colour is gradually being added to certain areas of the render. You can try different values, if desired.

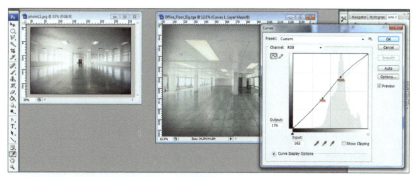

Adding points to the RGB Channel Curve

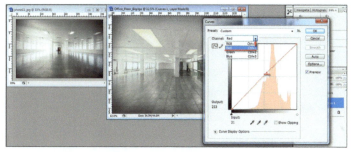

Adding points to the Red Channel Curve

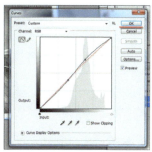

Curves final result

Ensure that this new adjustment layer is below the "vignetting" layer.
It's good practise to name Photoshop layers according to their respective tasks. Rename the "Curves" layer as "brightness & red tint".

Choosing the Layer Properties

5. To do so, simply right click on the layer, and choose the "Layer Properties" option from the list. You can also change its colour, if desired. Professionals often colour code layers by relevance i.e.red=important yellow= less important ; etc.)

6. Change the "Levels" layer name to "vignetting" and change its colour to red.

To closely match the floor of the render with the photo reference, simply open the "brightness & red tint" layer, by double clicking on its icon.

Renaming and changing the layer colour

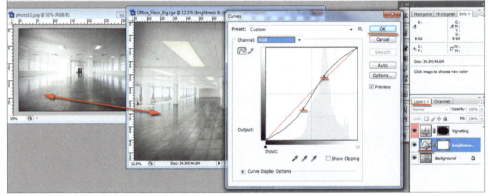

In the curves dialog, move down the lower point of the "RGB" curve. This action will darken the floor surface, in a balanced and realistic way. It's good practice to continuously evaluated colours, brightness level; etc.

Ajusting the Curves to match the floor of the Photo reference

3.4 Hue/Saturation

The next step is to try to balance the colour prominence of certain objects in the scene.

1. Add the "Hue /Saturation" adjustment layer by choosing it from the list.

Adding the Hue/Saturation adjustment layer

2. Its dialog should pop up. Instead of controlling the image colours globally through the "Master" option; we will do it through specific colours. Choose the "Green" colour from the edit list.

Hue/Saturation dialog

Also, you can pick the colour directly from the image, by hovering over with the cursor in the relevant area, and clicking on the desired area of the image.

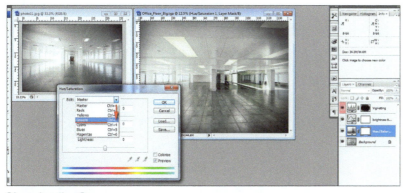

Choosing the Greens

3. In the "Saturation" function, reduce its value to about -30. The green areas of the image are gradually reduced now. You may also try different values if desired.

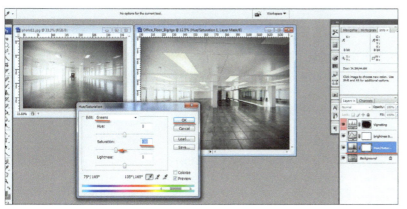

Editing the Greens

3.5 Glow

Next, we are going to add a bit of glow to the ceiling lights and the windows

Color Range

1. Open the "Object ID" render element under the name of "Office_Floor_AO_Object ID".

2. To select all the ceiling light colour IDs, click on the "Select" tab from the main toolbar. In the dropdown list, choose the "Color Range" option.

3. In the "Color Range" dialog, select the "Eye Dropper" tool, and select the ceiling light colour ID in the image.

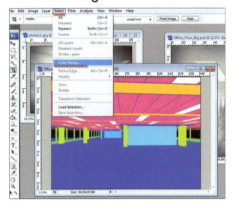

Choosing Color Range

Save Selection

Now is time to save this selection in the main working file.

1. While the selection is on, click the "Select" tab and choose the "Save Selection" option from the dropdown list.

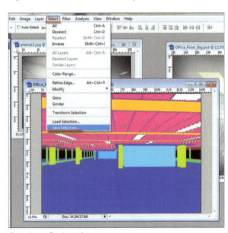

Saving Selection

4. All equal/similar colour IDs should be selected automatically. Click "OK" to close the dialog.

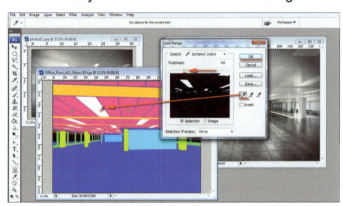

Selecting the colour with the Eye Dropper tool

Selected colours

2. Its dialog should appear. In the "Document" group, choose the appropriate document "Destination" to save the selection into(i.e. "office_floor_Big").

3. Save the new selection, and name it as "ceiling lights". This is one of many reasons why it's very useful to save render elements.

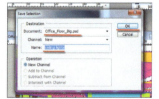

Save Selection dialog

4. Repeat the previous steps to save the window areas and name it accordingly (i.e. windows).

5. Back in the main document, open the channels' tab.
Select the "ceiling lights" channel, by holding down the "Ctrl" key and clicking its channel.

Enabling the saved Channel

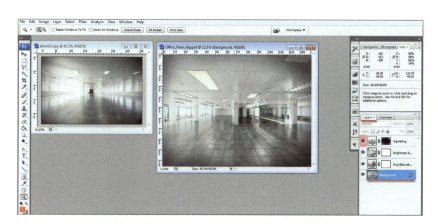

Selecting the Background layer

6. While the selection is still on; in the "Layers" tab, select the "Background" layer.

7. Copy and paste the selection by using the "Ctrl+C" keys to copy and "Ctrl+V" to paste the layer.
Name this new layer "ceiling glow", and change its layer colour to blue.

Ceiling Glow layer

Gaussian Blur

To emulate the glow on the copied layer, we are going to add the "Gaussian Blur" filter.

1. Click on the "Filter" tab, in main toolbar.

2. On the dropdown list, choose the "Gaussian Blur" filter.

Choosing Gaussian Blur filter

3. In the "Gaussian Blur" dialog, set its radius to about 7.0. You may try different values, if desired.

Setting the Gaussian Radius to 7

4. Back in the "Layer" document, change the blending mode to "Hard Mix" type. This blending mode seemed to have worked best. However, you may try a different one.

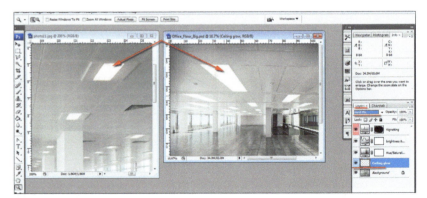

Usind Hard Mix blending mode

You may also try different levels of layer opacity to see what works best. Repeat the previous steps to add glow to the window.

Add Layer Mask

Next we are going to add randomness to the brightness of the ceiling lights.

1. While the "ceiling glow" layer is still selected, click on the "Add Layer Mask" button to create a mask.

2. As previously done, select the layer mask and enable the brush tool(B). Set the brush size to about 400,and the opacity to about 7%.

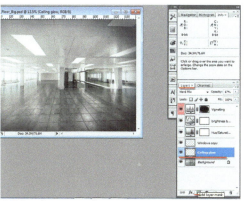

Adding layer mask

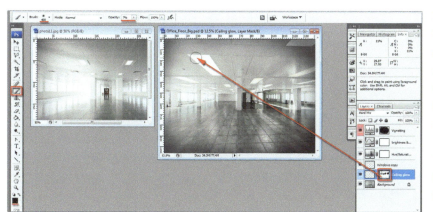

Masking out areas with the Brush tool and Layer mask

3. Ensure to have a black & white background/foreground colour swatch and begin brushing around the desired areas. Switch between the black & white background/foreground colour swatch(X) to add or omit areas.

The final result should be, random brightness levels of ceiling lights throughout the surface.

3.6 Chromatic Aberration

The next final stage is to add the chromatic aberration effect. This effect often adds a lot of realism to an image, when applied with subtlety.

Duplicating the Document

1. Duplicate the main document, by right clicking on top of it and choosing the "Duplicate" option from the pop up list.

Duplicate Image dialog

2. In the "Layer" tab of the new document, disable/hide the "vignetting" layer. Followed by flattening the document.

To flatten the document, simply right click on one of the document layers and choose the "Flatten Image" option. Also, accept to discard the hidden layers.

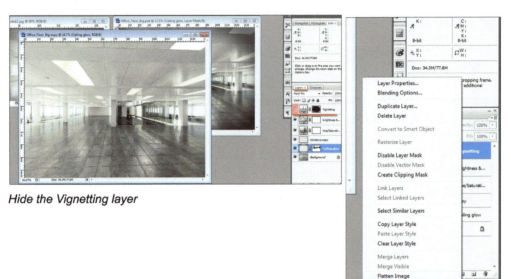

Hide the Vignetting layer

Flatten Image option

3. Before we start shifting channels, first zoom in to the document at 100%.

Or simply type in 100% at the bottom left part of the document. This action is necessary to prevent pixels from being shifted by more than 1.0.

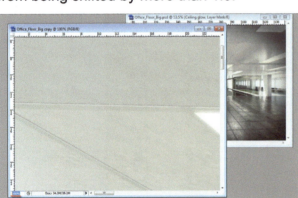

Document at 100%

4. Open the "Channels" tab and select the "Red" channel from the list.

5. Enable the move tool (V) and nudge upwards once, with the arrow key, so only one pixel is shifted.

6. Select the "Green" channel and nudge once downwards with the arrow key, so only one pixel is shifted.

7. Finally, select the "Blue" channel and nudge it to the left once, with the arrow key.

Nudging the Red channel up

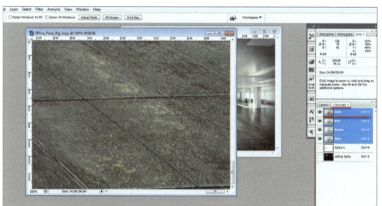

Returning to RGB channel

8. Now select the top "RGB" channel to return to colour mode and open the "Layers" tab. The result should be a slightly colourful image.

Close up of shifted channels (colourful)

Duplicating the Document

9. Select the main document with layers and duplicate it again.

10. Next, select all layers apart from the "vignetting". Right click and choose to "Merge Layers".

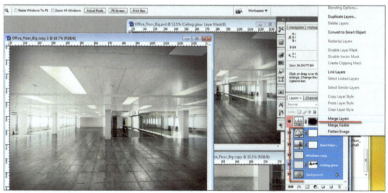

Merging Layers

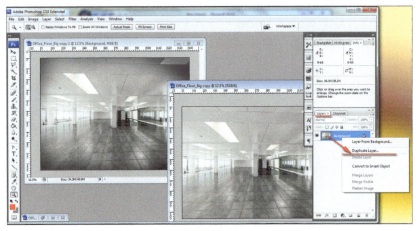

Duplicating the Layer

11. Select the document with the shifted channels (i.e. chromatic aberration).
Pick its background layer. Right click and choose to "Duplicate" the layer.

12. In the "Duplicate layer" dialog, choose the "Destination" of the layer to be in the document under the name of "office_floor_big copy 2". Also, name the new document "CA" (i.e. chromatic aberration).

Selecting the CA layer

Renaming and setting the Layer destination

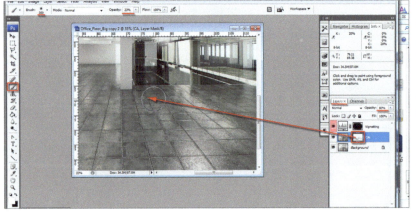

Masking out areas with the Brush Tool and Layer mask

13. Add a Layer mask to the CA layer and start brushing out to help control its prominence. Use some of the techniques highlighted earlier.

Also, you may want to decrease the layer opacity values.

The final result should be a very subtle CA (chromatic aberration).

Additionally, tweak further with the "vignetting" layer using some of the techniques highlighted earlier. And perhaps bring the Ambient Occlusion render to be overlaid on top of the base image using some of the blending layer modes.

Finally, try decreasing the height of the image by cropping out the upper area.

Reducing the Vignetting opacity

Final Result: Photo Reference & Office Rendering

www.ingramcontent.com/pod-product-compliance
Lightning Source LLC
Chambersburg PA
CBHW041420050326
40689CB00002B/587

9781467962094